The life and times of the Stockholm Conference on the Human Environment

With an introduction
by Maurice Strong, Director-General, U.N. environmental agency

THE PLOT
TO SAVE
THE WORLD

Wade Rowland

CLARKE, IRWIN & COMPANY LIMITED, TORONTO/VANCOUVER/1973

1 2 3 4 5   BP   77 76 75 74 73

Printed in Canada

Contents

Acknowledgments

I am indebted to many people for the help they have provided in assembling the material for this book — in particular to Norman Avery who was press-relations officer with the Canadian delegation to the Stockholm conference and to members of the legal division of the Canadian Department of External Affairs. I hasten to add that none is in any way responsible for any errors of fact or interpretation that may have crept into these pages: that responsibility is all my own. Finally I must acknowledge with affection the research, editing and translating assistance of Sarah Lea Altose, without whose help the book could never have been written.

To my parents

Introduction

Four years ago the General Assembly unanimously decided to convene the United Nations Conference on the Human Environment. That conference was held in Stockholm in June of 1972; the results represent the culmination of a long process of preparation and discussion involving almost all the nations of the world; the United Nations family; and countless other organizations—both governmental and non-governmental — and individuals with deep concern in this matter.

The conference brought together governments of 114 nations which met together in a spirit of trusteeship for all life on this planet and for life in the future; they discharged their solemn duty in an atmosphere of mutual respect, understanding, and sympathy — bound together by the knowledge that unless we conquer our divisions, our greeds, our inhibitions, and our fears, they will conquer us.

Stockholm launched a new liberation movement — liberation from man's thralldom to the new destructive forces which he, himself, has created. It also brought new force and determination to our drive for liberation from the continuing evils of mass poverty, economic and social injustice, racial prejudice, and the technologies of modern warfare which constitute such grave insults to the dignity of mankind and the greatest barriers to the achievement of a decent human environment for all.

The preparatory process and the conference, built on the pioneering work of so many, gave us new insights and perspectives and stirred new excitement and hope. Above all, it provided a practical basis for the realization of that hope — the essential framework for intergovernmental action and intensified public support for such action. These were the principal objectives envisaged by the General Assembly in convening the conference. Stockholm was both the culmination of the preparatory process and the beginning of the action process. The momentum evidenced by Stockholm has been carried forward since the conference in the actions of national governments, intergovernmental and non-governmental organizations, including the scientific community. But this is still only the beginning.

Perhaps the most striking feature of the preparatory process and the conference was this — the realization that the environmental issues are inextricably linked with all other factors in contemporary world politics; that we urgently require not only a new perception of man's relationship with the natural world, but with man's relationship with man; that the problems of the rich cannot be seen in isolation from those of the poor; that in all respects we inhabit Only One Earth.

As we now take up our work, what do we see as the prospect for Planet Earth?

In a limited sense, the answer is that nobody knows for sure. This is not the time to remind you of inescapable statistics nor of the scale of the revolutions through which we are living — exploding population, galloping urbanization that concentrates and deepens every impact of people on their environment, rising energy consumption as an index of the steadily increasing material claims, uses, wastes and effluents of the new and growing technological order.

None would deny the vast benefits to man that this new technological order has produced, nor the improvements it has made possible in many aspects of the environment. But we know that our activities have created serious imbalances. We know, too, that not only each society, but the world as a whole must achieve a better balance among the major elements that determine the level and quality of life it can provide for its members — population and its distribution, available resources and their exploitation, and pressures placed on the life systems that sustain it.

There is much difference of opinion in the scientific community over the severity of the environmental problem and whether doom is imminent or, indeed, inevitable. But one does not have to accept the inevitability of environmental catastrophe to accept the possibility of catastrophe. We need subscribe to no doomsday threat to be convinced that we cannot — we dare not — wait for all the evidence to be in. Time is no ally here unless we make it one.

Whether the crisis is, in a physical sense, just around the corner or well over the horizon cannot obscure the fact that we have a policy crisis on our hands right now. We need only look at the unintended results of past decisions.

No one decided as a deliberate matter to poison our polluted and dying waterways.

No one decided as a deliberate matter to destroy millions of acres of productive soil through erosion, salination, contamination and the intrusion of deserts.

No one decided as a deliberate matter to dehumanize life in the great cities of the world with crowding, pollution and noise for the more fortunate and with the degrading squalor of slums for the rest.

We did not intend to do this, but this is what we did!

Clearly, man has been making his decisions on too narrow a base and in too short a time horizon.

It is this that requires a new approach and a broader perspective.

What, then, are the central implications of this approach? Stockholm has confirmed that the environment issue cannot be conceived in narrow defensive or parochial terms, but in the possibilities it opens up to bring new energies, new perspectives, and a new will to the resolution of the fundamental imbalances and conflicts which continue to afflict mankind. For the developing countries, environmental considerations add a new dimension to the concept of development — involving not merely the avoidance of newly perceived dangers, but the realization of promising new opportunities. For the richer nations, it provides a dramatic illustration of the new interdependencies which the technological society has created, and new reasons for a deeper and sustained commitment to a more equitable sharing of its benefits with the developing world. Thus, there can be no fundamental conflict between development and environment; they are integral and indivisible.

The central theme of our age is interdependence — the interdependence of all the elements which sustain life on this planet; the interdependence of man with these elements; the interdependence of the natural physical systems with man's needs and aspirations; and, most of all, man's interdependence with man.

This will be achieved not by a denial of national sovereignty but by new and more effective means of enabling nations to exercise this sovereignty collectively where they can no longer exercise it effectively alone. We are not moving towards an ephemeral supra-nationalism, but towards a wider, deeper and more realistic conception of the responsibilities of individual nation-states towards their neighbours, and towards the preservation and enhancement of all life on this planet.

The long-range importance of Stockholm will be evidenced in the kind of actions to which it gave rise in changing the perceptions, the attitudes and practices which are responsible for our present dilemma.

We must recognize that the difficult choices remain to be made, and that they cannot be made solely by governments or international organizations. They must rest on the willingness and ability of people to see that the relentless pursuit of narrow concepts of individual and national interests, which has done so much to push us towards higher material standards, now constitutes a grave peril to our physical as well as our moral survival.

I do not believe these forces need be extinguished, but they must be modified, controlled and directed by an overriding commitment to the common interests and to the kind of co-operative behaviour needed to ensure the well-being of the whole human family.

Stockholm has shown that this is not an impossible dream. It has shown — both in the preparatory process and at the Conference itself — that the United Nations system, contrary to the many doubts which have been expressed about it, can face up to the problems of our day and time. It has shown the depth of experience and knowledge which it can mobilize, and it has shown that these diverse elements *can* work together harmoniously and creatively when presented with the challenge of achieving a common goal. And I am convinced that the system can respond to the new responsibilities to work towards solutions for the environmental problems of our Only One Earth.

MAURICE F. STRONG

New York, 1972.

Prologue

The usual round of self-congratulatory speeches signalled the close of the first United Nations conference on the human environment early in the afternoon of June 16, 1972. Those of the haggard delegates from 114 nations who had stuck it out to the end rose from their desks in the main conference room of Stockholm's quietly modernistic *Folkets Hus* and began stuffing their black polyvinyl U.N. briefcases with that day's ration of the 40 tons of official documents churned out during the meeting. They had reason to be weary: in just under two weeks they had sifted through hundreds of pages of recommendations, resolutions, and declarations touching on nearly every aspect of man's relation to his environment. They had succeeded also in conjuring up a not altogether incoherent programme as a first step towards a more rational adjustment of that relation.

At a campsite on the outskirts of the city, meanwhile, a colourful collection of Woodstock graduates, former Merry Pranksters and other assorted acid-heads, eco-freaks, save-the-whalers, doomsday mystics, poets and hangers-on were striking their tents and preparing to split — for Topeka, Vancouver, Nepal, Amsterdam, London ... wherever whim and precarious finances would take them. They had come to Stockholm — mostly from the U.S. — to help the conference "get it on", to try to imbue the historic debates with the spirit of transcendentalism and humility before nature that the American counter-culture had lately been espousing. Their failure to call up any noticeable, constructive influence on the conference proceedings need not have worried them, since the meeting, through its own momentum and sense of purpose, had far exceeded the expectations of even the most optimistic observers. Street theatre, rock concerts and dress-up parades had proven unnecessary, though entertaining encouragements.

And at other downtown meeting halls the other non-U.N. "outer conferences" were disassembling their displays and demonstration booths. The Marxists were holding yet another press conference from which, again, selected journalists were to find themselves excluded without explanation, and the various unlabelled radicals and concerned ob-

1

servers continued the arguments that their official meetings had been unable to resolve.

All of them — from those who wore headbands to the conventional, concerned liberals, to those who wore armbands — had worked hard during those two weeks for a common concern. But none had worked harder than the diplomats themselves. Old U.N. hands agreed that it was probably the hardest-working high-level international conference within memory. One of the most telling pieces of trivia to emerge from the 13 days of negotiation was that Stockholm night-spot managers, stocking up on wine and liquor in anticipation of a bonanza, had been left after it was all over with storerooms still jammed to the rafters. The expected rush by 1,200 official delegates, and as many journalists and pseudo-journalists who had somehow contrived to get press credentials (not to mention another couple of thousand interested observers), had somehow failed to materialize. Scarcely a ripple had been raised in attendance figures at the city's notorious sex-show cabarets and pornographic cinemas. Delegates were in the frustrating position of students faced with final examinations during the Stanley Cup play-offs. To their credit, an astonishingly large majority buckled down to work with hardly more than a wistful glance in the direction of Stockholm's more tantalizing delights. Perhaps the tone was set by the doggedly conscientious Chinese delegation; more likely, consciences were fortified by the knowledge that taxpayers back home were watching these particular meetings with a concerned interest seldom focused on such conferences in the past. Dimly perceived though it may have been, there was a broad and growing understanding among the peoples of the world that the Stockholm conference would see the first salvoes fired in what was likely to be one of the crucial political struggles in recorded history — a unique struggle, in which the fundamental interests of virtually every one of the Earth's 3.5 billion inhabitants would be intimately involved. It would be, in a very literal sense, a struggle to save the world.

The world's press, at first skeptical, was forced that day to concede that the conference had been a success. There was less agreement, however, on the exact nature of the meeting's achievements. Many, if not most, commentaries centred on two of the conference's more readily explainable decisions, to establish a global "Earthwatch" system and set up a new agency to control a greatly expanded U.N. environmental preservation programme.

Earthwatch was unquestionably an ambitious programme, and an essential first step to be taken in any worldwide environmental management scheme. The idea was to establish and maintain a system for continuous monitoring of the health of the lithosphere, hydrosphere and atmosphere throughout the world, and to support this system with internationally-based research and information-exchange programmes. Earthwatch would collect data on a global basis and feed it to a central location (the U.N.'s computer complex in Geneva) where it could be interpreted objectively to provide the international community with the information necessary for rational policy-making.

Many of the activities to be co-ordinated under the Earthwatch umbrella were already being undertaken by an assortment of more than thirty private, intergovernmental and non-governmental agencies. Among these were the World Meteorological Organization's World Weather Watch and the International Council of Scientific Unions' Global Atmospheric Research Programme; the International Oceanographic Commission's Global Investigation of Pollution in the Marine Environment; the Integrated Global Ocean Station System being developed jointly by the W.M.O. and I.O.C.; the continuing marine pollution assessment programme of the inter-agency Joint Group of Experts on the Scientific Aspects of Marine Pollution, supported by six different U.N. agencies; the Global Radiation Monitoring Programme of the U.N. Scientific Committee on the Effects of Atomic Radiation; and comparable programmes relating to food quality in the joint Food and Agriculture Organization–World Health Organization Codex Alimentarius Commission.[1]

The channelling of Earthwatch data through the computer centre in Geneva, where programmers could use newly-acquired techniques to make the fine semantic distinctions necessary for convenient searching of the machine's memory banks, would prove to have unsuspected advantages. As a bonus, the carefully-programmed computer would be capable of settling the time-consuming disagreements over word definitions that crop up invariably at international conferences, and to which the Stockholm meeting was by no means immune. During one day of negotiation a long delay was caused by an argument over whether "halted" and "checked" meant the same thing, and another occurred while delegates debated a French objection to the use of the word "nuisance" as too specifically Anglo-Saxon. In the latter case, discussions were able to resume only when a delegate from Uruguay intervened to point out that the derivation was from the French *nuire*. At future conferences, it would be left to the computer to sort out such problems.

The institutional arrangements that emerged from the conference provided for a vigorous and flexible body with a governing council of

54 nations and a strong secretariat. Its functions were to fall under four headings: knowledge acquisition and assessment (Earthwatch), environmental quality management (producing recommendations and guidelines, setting uniform national codes, preparing treaties, conventions, etc.), the prevention and settlement of disputes involving environmental issues and, finally, the mobilization of international support to help less developed nations play a significant role in the performance of the first two functions. The new agency would be financed mainly by a voluntary fund, targeted at $100 million over the first five years of its existence: by the end of the conference there seemed little doubt that this goal would be reached.

Unfortunately, the new organization was granted its broad powers only over the collective dead bodies of the chiefs of a number of other U.N. specialized agencies — notably F.A.O., the International Atomic Energy Agency, W.H.O. and the U.N. Educational, Social and Cultural Organization — strenuously opposed to the creation of any new body that would cut into their prestige and areas of responsibility. It seemed probable that the environment agency would have to endure at least two or three years of inter-agency haggling before the dust settled and one could determine just how powerful and influential it would eventually become.

While the press rallied to applaud these important initiatives, the fact remained that the crucial problems facing the Stockholm delegates were murkier ones, monsters from the realm of international politics and international law: the hardiest adversaries of the plot to save the world.

NOTE

1. To simplify administration, Earthwatch's programme was broken down into four categories: evaluation (including forecasting), research, monitoring, and information exchange. Evaluation programmes would be expected to identify environmental concerns of major international significance, determine the state of knowledge in each area, and assess risks so as to derive guidelines for international standards. They would also be expected to perform a continuous review of other programmes, identifying gaps and facilitating co-ordination and smooth information exchange. Research, of course, was urgently needed in virtually every area of environmental concern. The monitoring programme was designed to provide some of the basic data needed for that research. The first job would be to conduct a series of baseline surveys to establish the state of various environmental systems. A number of global observation networks were to be established for keeping watch on specific variables, including the make-up of the atmosphere and related climate changes, the world's forest cover, and the state of its fresh-water supply. Earthwatch would also work towards establishing an international warning system for natural disasters. Information exchange programmes were centred around another creation of the conference, the International Referral Service for Sources of Environmental

Information. The service was conceived as a kind of switchboard for the exchange of information between governments, universities, industries, regional economic commissions trying to plan aid programmes, small farming or research groups in developing areas looking for help, and other agencies and organizations either needing information or in a position to supply it. Its headquarters would be at the U.N. computer complex in Geneva.

For a Living World, Not the Garden of Eden

Judging by published accounts of its first few days, the United Nations environmental conference in Stockholm is developing as a combination of cloud-nine idealism, trendy New Left posturing and, somewhere in there, serious concern with the question of what is going on in the delicate equation of Man and his life-supporting world. The danger is apparent that the two-week meeting may produce only a sheaf of grand resolutions that will be easily forgotten because of their impracticability or, alternatively, that it will dissolve in cynicism and recrimination if realistic economics are asserted too strongly. What is needed to prevent either of these results is cool assessment of the existing knowledge of the environment and constant awareness that the primary objective is human welfare, not the restoration of the Garden of Eden . . .

The one unreservedly commendable recommendation before the conference is to establish a world-wide agency under U.N. auspices to collect and correlate the available scientific information about environmental control, and possibly to initiate its own research programmes where knowledge is found to be lacking. The world is only at the beginning of a clear understanding of its pollution and conservation problems. There are many ideas, good, bad and indifferent; they all need greater discipline of facts.

Lead editorial in the *Globe and Mail* (Toronto), June 7, 1972.

Chapter one

Forecasts and blueprints

Perhaps it was no mere coincidence that this first high-level international conference on the preservation of the human environment met during the same year a book bearing the unfashionably pedestrian title *The Limits to Growth*[1] made its appearance. Published just weeks before the United Nations' historic Stockholm conference opened to mixed reviews, the little book set forth what it called "the predicament of mankind" in terms so clear, and so weighted with the authority of the most modern systems-dynamics techniques, that only the most belligerently myopic of readers was able to avoid some chill of apprehension for the future of man on this planet.

The book was the first substantial fruit of four years' labour by members of the Club of Rome, an informal gathering of about seventy European scientists, educators, economists, industrialists, and national and international civil servants. The group met first in the Italian capital during April, 1968, at the instigation of Dr. Aurelio Peccei, an industrialist and economist, consultant to Fiat and Olivetti. At that meeting they set themselves the imposing task of analyzing the present problems and possible future options facing man as he approaches the finite limits to his biological and industrial expansion on Earth.

The pattern for research that formed the basis for *The Limits to Growth* began to take final shape during the summer of 1970, when a special Club of Rome committee met for two weeks in Cambridge, Massachusetts with Professor Jay W. Forrester, a systems-dynamics analyst with the Massachusetts Institute of Technology. During those two weeks Forrester demonstrated the first working computer model of the functioning of key aspects of the human environment.[2] The model dealt with the complex interrelationships among five principal variables: population, capital investment (including food production and medical care), natural resources reserves, pollution, and an estimate of quality of life based on such factors as food per capita, material goods and crowding. Forrester, more interested at that stage in the functioning of the model than in any predictions it might make, drew one major conclusion that seemed to have such universal application to man's policies for managing his environment that it might almost be termed a law of nature: virtually all short-term, piecemeal remedies for environmental problems lead to long-term deterioration. The lesson has been summarized by Nobel prize-winner Dennis Gabor as "short-term remedy — long-term deterioration", a rule of thumb of particular significance in democracies where officials are elected for four- or five-year terms and are thus obliged to seek short-term remedies to ensure re-election.[3] As for "the predicament of mankind", a large number of computer runs exploring our current situation and various policy options for the future led Forrester to the conclusion that man's golden age had already arrived, and the quality of life on Earth was likely to decline continuously in the foreseeable future as a result of pollution, crowding, hunger, disease, and so on. Policy options which assumed indefinite growth in either population or capital investment (including agricultural investment) implied grisly disaster on the worldwide scale, in the forms of soaring pollution and a precipitous decline in population from famine and disease. The only hope offered by the computer model lay in policy decisions which would immediately reduce world birth rates by 50 per cent, cut pollution per unit of output by 50 per cent, and reduce capital investment (including agricultural investment) by 40 per cent. For those who survived the three-per-cent-per-capita cut in food supplies these policies implied, the future would be a relatively placid one in which our quality of life would reach unprecedented heights in a world where most resource-consuming kinds of growth had been brought to a halt.

The Club of Rome group, led by Dr. Dennis L. Meadows[4] and financed by a grant from the Volkswagen Foundation, relied heavily on the systems-analysis techniques developed by Prof. Forrester in evolving their own model of the factors which they believe ultimately place limits on growth on this planet: population, agricultural production, natural resources, industrial production and pollution. As their model was essentially a refinement of Forrester's, with variations in emphasis here and there, it is not surprising that it gave similar results. From the point of view of the environmentalist, however, the Club of Rome model was more interesting and immediately relevant, because it tended to examine policy options on the basis of more realistic assumptions.

One of the major achievements of *The Limits to Growth* was to bring home, once and for all, the breathtaking perils of exponential growth. This concept is summarized nicely in a French children's riddle recounted in the book. Suppose a farmer owns a pond in which a lily is growing. The plant doubles in size each day, so that if its growth is not checked it will eventually cover the entire surface of the pond, squeezing out all other life in the water. For many days the plant seems to remain small, but eventually the farmer notices that it is covering half the pond. He decides that he will soon have to cut back its growth. How long does he have to act? Until the next day, of course.

The key to exponential growth, then, lies in "doubling time". A simple mathematical formula will provide the doubling time of any number that is multiplying at a constant rate. The following graph shows the relationship between growth rate expressed as a percentage per year and the amount of time it takes for any given sum to double its size. If we are talking about money in the bank, for instance, the chart shows that a sum of money left in the bank at four per cent interest will double in 18 years. The growth of any thing that is allowed to multiply unchecked can be expressed in similar terms.

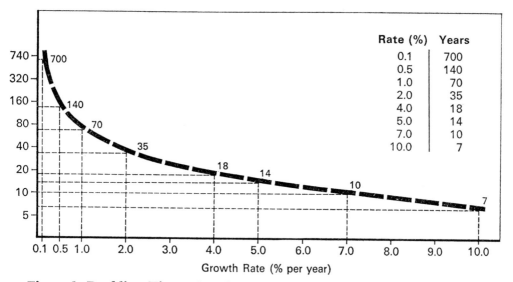

Rate (%)	Years
0.1	700
0.5	140
1.0	70
2.0	35
4.0	18
5.0	14
7.0	10
10.0	7

Growth Rate (% per year)

Figure 1, Doubling Times: Canada's population in 1967 was growing at about one per cent a year, for a doubling time of 70 years. Current world population growth rate is about two per cent a year for a doubling time of 35 years.

To determine the rate of growth and thus the doubling time of any system, it is necessary to know which elements cause or encourage growth and which work to slow that growth. These two factors are sometimes known, respectively, as "positive feedback" and "negative feedback". In the case of human population growth, for example, the birth rate provides the positive feedback and the death rate the negative feedback. To find the rate of growth of a population, one simply subtracts the death rate from the birth rate. In 1967, Canada's birth rate was 1.82 per cent and the death rate .74 per cent, giving a rate of increase in population of $1.82 - .74 = 1.08$ per cent per year. As the graph shows, this gives the Canadian population a doubling time of roughly 70 years, barring immigration.

A second important aspect of exponential growth is that the impact of the growth that takes place during each doubling period tends to increase suddenly and dramatically as time goes by. The result, as the story of the lily pond suggests, can be rather like the experience of the man who jumped off the Empire State Building and as he passed the 25th storey said: "So far, so good." This explosive aspect of exponential growth can lead policy makers into all kinds of pitfalls, for often **a** problem that seems merely serious one day has become overwhelming

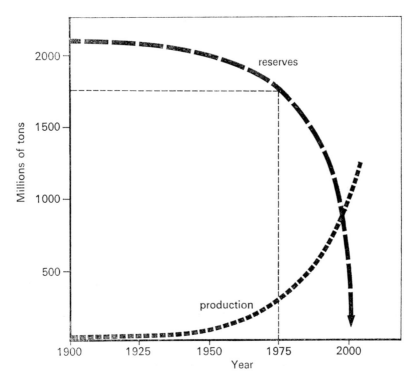

Figure 2: The exploitation of a typical (but hypothetical) resource. Production, growing exponentially at approximately seven per cent per year, causes a concurrent exponential decrease in reserves. In 1975, just 25 years before the point where reserves equal only one year's production (in the year 2000) world reserves of the resource have been depleted by only 12½ per cent.

before there is time to act. Today's serious problem of finding enough food to feed the world's 3.5 billion people will become tomorrow's desperate crisis of how to feed double that number — and "tomorrow" is only 35 years away at the present world population-growth rate of about two per cent.

By the same token, reserves of non-renewable resources such as petroleum and other minerals can seem staggeringly large when seen in simple arithmetical terms, but they may turn out to be soberingly tiny in the light of an exponentially-growing rate of exploitation. Known world reserves of aluminum ore are currently estimated at 1.17 billion tons. If the use of the metal continued indefinitely at today's rate, these reserves would last approximately 100 years. However, the rate of use of aluminum is increasing exponentially (as is the rate of use of virtually all other resources) at about 6.4 per cent a year. Reserves will in fact last only 31 years assuming, of course, that prices or other outside factors do not act to reduce the rate of consumption before that time.[5] An increase in the price of aluminum resulting from its growing scarcity would naturally lead to increased recycling, more intensive exploration, and the exploitation of known low-yield ore bodies that were previously uneconomic. If we make allowance for these facts by multiplying today's known reserves by, say, five, a few minutes of calculation demonstrate that aluminum reserves will still last only 55 years. The chart on page 14 gives similar figures for other resources (statistics supplied by the U.S. Bureau of Mines).

The crucial lesson to be learned from these figures is that exponential growth has the effect of drastically foreshortening our expectations. If the rate of increase in the use of coal were to drop to zero today — that is, if we continued indefinitely to use exactly as much coal per year as we will this year — reserves would last for 2,300 years to come. Exponential growth of 4.1 per cent per year, as the chart shows, has shortened this expectation to somewhere in the neighbourhood of 111 years.[6] One need scarcely point out that depletion of resource reserves in the real world depends on factors immensely more complicated than merely the projected rate of growth in use and known reserves. With this in mind the Club of Rome committee set up a computer run which considered such additional factors as extraction costs, expected advances in mining technology, and substitution of other materials. The resource chosen for the test was chromium. Based on this more complex, realistic data, the computer's prediction for the life of known chromium reserves was 125 years, or 30 years longer than suggested by

Resource	Projected average rate of growth (% per year) in use	Number of years known reserves will last at this rate of growth	Number of years 5x known reserves would last
Aluminum	6.4	31	55
Chromium	2.6	95	154
Coal	4.1	111	150
Cobalt	1.5	60	148
Copper	4.6	21	48
Gold	4.1	9	29
Iron	1.8	93	173
Lead	2.0	21	64
Manganese	2.9	46	94
Mercury	2.6	13	41
Molybdenum	4.5	34	65
Natural gas	4.7	22	49
Nickel	3.4	53	96
Petroleum	3.9	20	50
Platinum group	3.8	47	85
Silver	2.7	13	42
Tin	1.1	15	61
Tungsten	2.5	28	72
Zinc	2.9	18	50

the simple calculations in the chart above. Assuming a twofold increase in known reserves extended the exhaustion point by only 20 years, to 145.

The committee concluded from its examination of resource reserves: "Given present resource-consumption rates and the projected increase in these rates, the great majority of the currently important non-renewable resources will be extremely costly 100 years from now. This statement remains true regardless of the most optimistic assumptions about undiscovered reserves, technological advances, substitution, or recycling, as long as the demand for resources continues to grow exponentially."[7]

As population soars under the influence of a high birth rate coupled with a falling death rate, and as resource use, responding to rising industrial output in most of the world's nations, describes its exponential upward curve, it is not surprising to find pollution following close behind. And, in fact, where pollutants have been measured accurately over a long enough period, this has been shown to be the case (Figures 3-6). No one knows just where the upward sloping curve of pollution levels meets the downward curve of the Earth's ability to absorb contaminants without serious damage to the delicate living networks of the biosphere. Nor does anyone know where the upward limit is to the exponential growth of population. But to those with a clear idea of the snowballing nature of the problems of resource depletion, pollution and population, the much-quoted 1969 statement by U Thant, then secretary-general of the United Nations, did not seem unjustifiably bleak.

> I do not wish to seem overdramatic, but I can only conclude from the information that is available to me as secretary-general that the members of the United Nations have perhaps ten years left in which to subordinate their ancient quarrels and launch a global partnership to curb the arms race, to improve the human environment, to defuse the population explosion, and to supply the required momentum to development efforts. If such a global partnership is not forged within the next decade, then I very much fear that the problems I have mentioned will have reached such staggering proportions that they will be beyond our capacity to control.

Like Forrester before them, the Club of Rome special committee concluded that global calamity is likely to be avoided, or at least minimized, if action is taken during the next few decades to halt population growth and begin turning back the numbers to somewhere around today's figure, as well as to stop the exponential increase in resource-consuming industrial output. In other words, they joined Forrester in calling for a steady-state world economy — one that is in long-term equilibrium with the rest of the global ecosystem. Technology, the committee decided, will prove indispensable in augmenting food production and reducing pollution, and even, perhaps, slowing resource depletion through increased efficiencies. But to rely on technology alone, without taking urgent action to stop exponential growth, would be courting certain disaster in the form of a collapse of one or more of the systems sustaining human life on this planet. Peccei himself summarized the results of the computer study in a speech entitled "Human Settlements" which he delivered to a distinguished lecture series run in conjunction with the U.N. conference in Stockholm.

> The main conclusion to be drawn from this study is that equilibrium within the human system and between it and its environment will anyhow be re-established. Evidently, it is in our collective interest rationally to plan for it, even at the cost of heretofore unimaginable sacrifices, and not to wait for forces outside our control to settle it — which will probably occur at the cost of tremendous human suffering. On the other hand society in equi-

librium does not mean stagnation. Non-material-consuming and non-environment-degrading activities may be pursued indefinitely — such as education, art, music, religion, scientific research, sport, social interactions and most service activities.

What we have to consider here is the perspective of collapse, because it will render at least dubious the possibility of further human settlement.

Collapse may happen because humans will spread their presence

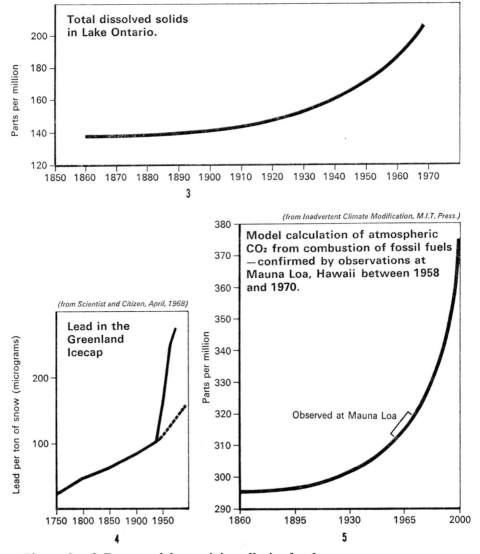

Figures 3 to 6: Exponential growth in pollution levels

and activity so greatly that forces in the planetary ecosystem will expel or destroy man as a noxious intruder who upsets the ever-changing but always harmonious web of life. Should this happen, it will mean that *homo sapiens*, the last of the big animal species to appear on the globe, would prove to be a mistake in the biosphere's evolutionary process, a mistake that the delicate but stubborn mechanisms of life would move to correct even if this meant their going back a few million years — just a moment in the eons

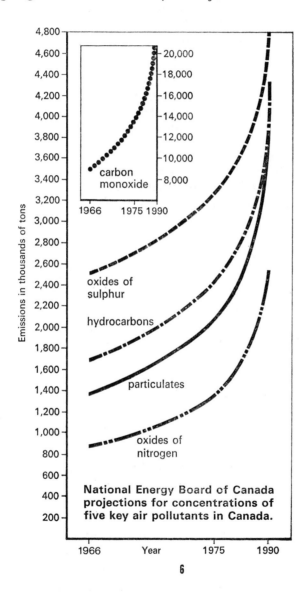

National Energy Board of Canada projections for concentrations of five key air pollutants in Canada.

6

of time: suffice it to think that the dinosaurs reigned for 200 million years. Life will then start again in another direction, free from the danger of producing another freak of the human type.

Collapse may also occur because man dissipates the non-renewable resources of the planet, which are necessary for the technical society he has engineered. These resources have been accumulated in successive geological ages during billions of years before the age of man. But man, trapped by his cultural fallacy that he is king of the earth — not just a tiny part and parcel of nature — wants all these resources for himself, calling them "the common heritage of mankind". He is, however, inconsistent even with his philosophy, because he squanders and uses up many of these resources within the short span of a few generations, converting them into waste and pollution, thus depriving the next generations of the riches to which they are supposed to have equal title, and leaving them instead the legacy of an unspeakable mess to clean up.

Collapse may also be caused by war and civil strife — if, for instance, the next wave of human population which will invade the planet in the next three or four decades does not find a place to settle or the means to satisfy its needs. This grim alternative has to be considered with all due attention . . .

Predictably, criticism of the Club of Rome report was prompt in coming. Unfortunately, however, most of what has appeared to date has been, to put the most charitable face on it, oblique. One who rose to scorn *The Limits to Growth* as "sheer nonsense" was Sir Solly Zuckerman, who has recently renewed some of his wartime fame as a scientific advisor to the British government by becoming a vocal naysayer of ecological concern, and has apparently managed to live down an earlier study of the behaviour of apes that was a near-classic of scientific fallibility. Zuckerman told his audience in the Stockholm distinguished lecture series: "The only kind of exponential growth with which the book [*The Limits to Growth*] does not deal, and which I for one believe is a fact, is the growth of human knowledge and of the increase in the kind of understanding with which we can imbue our efforts as we see to it that our increasing numbers do not become incompatible with a better life . . ."

The statement scarcely required comment, since members of the Club of Rome would be among the last to deny the role of knowledge and understanding in the eventual solution of the problems it had described. In fact a few minutes later, Zuckerman himself made the only relevant observation in stating that "the alarm which we now experience in fact comes from our increased knowledge of what we are doing." The British scientist was firm in his faith in man's ability to find solutions to environmental problems without resorting to such drastic measures as reduction of exponential growth rates: "For example, if it were an ineluctable scientific conclusion that the use of supersonic civil transport would irrevocably wreck the ozone layer which overlies the atmosphere, can we seriously imagine that we would not find ways of inhibiting the use of such an aircraft as our knowledge of their secondary effects — if any — became more apparent? What are we — ants, lemmings, or rational human beings?" A reply might have noted that the S.S.T. is here, and will be used by several of the world's airlines, in spite of the admitted fact that research has shown a distinct possibility that the ozone layer will be damaged.[8] The decision to go ahead with the S.S.T. in such circumstances of incomplete but troubling knowledge might seem, to an objective observer, more lemming-like than rational.

Other criticism, though maintaining a safer distance from possible charges of deliberate obscurantism, seemed no more constructive. Writing in *Commentary*,[9] London University research associate Rudolf Klein went to almost grotesque lengths to ignore the substance of the report (which he dismissed as "a matter for experts") and devoted his entire article to a critique of the book as a piece of "futurology" in the tradition of medieval prophecies of "approaching devastation by wind and storm, by drought and famine, pestilence and earthquake; often, indeed, a precise date was given for the impending catastrophe and when the Antichrist, the Red Dragon with Seven Heads and Ten Horns, or the Tyrant of the Last Days, would appear." Klein appeared not to have noticed a statement in the "commentary" section of the report: "The project was not intended as a piece of futurology. It was intended to be, and is, an analysis of current trends, of their influence on each other, and of their possible outcomes. Our goal was to provide warnings of potential world crisis if these trends are allowed to continue, and thus offer an opportunity to make changes in our political, economic and social systems to ensure that these crises do not take place." Dr. Peccei's brusqueness was understandable when he observed, to a Stockholm press conference, that many of *The Limits to Growth*'s assailants had apparently not bothered to read the book.

Word filtering out late in 1971 of the work being done by the Club of Rome was also responsible, along with more traditional ecological concern, for the drafting of another landmark document. *The Ecologist* magazine's "Blueprint for Survival"[10] hit the newsstands in January, 1972 — just six months before the Stockholm conference got under way — and raised a storm of controversy that spread to the British House of Commons and much of the rest of the English-speaking world. Thirty-six of Britain's leading scientists and thinkers lent their weight to the document with a statement that read: "The undersigned, without endorsing every detail, fully support the basic principles embodied in 'The Blueprint for Survival' ... both in respect of the analysis of the problems we face today, and the solutions proposed."

The Blueprint called for formation of a "movement for survival" which would try to exert sufficient political pressure to force British parliamentarians to adopt policies more in line with what its authors saw as the ecological realities of the 1970s. As a quasi-political document — a sort of manifesto — it left itself open to a much broader range of criticism than *The Limits to Growth*. No scientific delicacy veiled its urgent statement. "An examination of the relevant information," the authors wrote in a preface, "has impressed upon us the extreme gravity of the global situation today. For, if current trends are allowed to persist, the breakdown of society and the irreversible disruption of the life-support systems on this planet, possibly by the end of the century, certainly within the lifetimes of our children, are inevitable." The preface continued: "Governments, and ours is no exception, are either refusing to face the relevant facts, or are briefing their scientists in such a way that their seriousness is played down. Whatever the reason, no corrective measures of any consequence are being taken." The most "relevant" fact of all, the article stated, was that "the industrial way of life with its ethos of expansion ... is not sustainable. Its termination within the lifetime of someone born today is inevitable — unless it continues to be sustained for a while longer by an entrenched minority at the cost of imposing great suffering on the rest of mankind. We can be certain, however, that sooner or later it will end (only the precise time and circumstances are in doubt), and that it will do so in one of two ways: either against our will, in a succession of famines, epidemics, social crises and wars; or because we want it to — because we wish to create a society which will not impose hardship and cruelty upon our children — in a succession of thoughtful, humane and measured changes." The goal was a steady-state or "stable" society of the kind envisaged sketchily in *The Limits to Growth* — and also, more than a century earlier, by John Stuart Mill, in his *Principles of Political Economy* (1857):

> I cannot, therefore, regard the stationary state of capital and wealth with the unaffected aversion so generally manifested toward it by political economists of the old school. I am inclined to believe that it would be, on the whole, a very considerable improvement on our own condition. ... I confess I am not charmed with the ideal of life held out by those who think that the normal state of

human beings is that of struggling to get on; that the trampling, crushing, elbowing, and treading on each other's heels which forms the existing type of social life are the most desirable lot of human kind. ... The northern and middle states of America are a specimen of this stage of civilization in very favourable circumstances; and all that these advantages seem to have done for them ... is that the life of the whole of one sex is devoted to dollar hunting, and of the other to breeding dollar hunters.

I know not why it should be a matter of congratulation that persons who are already richer than anyone needs to be should have doubled their means of consuming things which give little or no pleasure except as a representative of wealth. ... It is only in the backward countries of the world that increased production is still an important object; in those most advanced, what is economically needed is a better distribution, of which one indispensable means is a stricter restraint on population. ... The density of population necessary to enable mankind to obtain, in the greatest degree, all the advantages both of co-operation and social intercourse, has, in all the most populous countries, been attained. ... It is not good for a man to be kept perforce at all times in the presence of his own species. ... Nor is there much satisfaction in contemplating a world with nothing left of the spontaneous activity of nature. ... If the Earth must lose that great portion of its pleasantness which it owes to things that the unlimited increase of wealth and population would extirpate from it for the mere purpose of enabling it to support a larger population, I sincerely hope, for the sake of posterity, that they will be content to be stationary long before necessity compels them to it.

It is scarcely necessary to remark that a stationary condition of capital and population implies no stationary state of human improvement. There would be as much scope as ever for all kinds of mental culture and moral and social progress; as much room for improving the Art of Living and much more likelihood of it being improved, when minds cease to be engrossed by the art of getting on.[11]

The Blueprint outlined an orchestrated series of changes which it saw as being necessary if the stationary state was to emerge, with its minimal disruptions of ecological systems, maximum conservation of energy and resources, zero population growth and less restrictive social system (see Appendix 1). The transformation, it was suggested, should take place in seven main operations, starting with a "control operation" to reduce ecological disruption as much as possible by technical means (anti-pollution technology), and followed by a "freeze operation" in which particularly damaging trends are halted. Next would come asystemic substitution by which the most dangerous components of those trends are replaced with short-term technological substitutes, as when DDT is replaced by Malathion or propoxur, or phosphates in detergents are replaced by, say, NTA. Following this would be systemic substitution, in which these technological substitutes are replaced by "natural" or self-regulating processes that either imitate or make non-disruptive use of natural environmental systems. Malathion, for example, used in the previous stage to replace the more harmful DDT, would now be replaced by biological pest-control measures which rely on natural insect predators.

The next stage would be the "invention, promotion and application" of alternative technologies which are less energy- and resource-consuming — a switch to what Buckminster Fuller would call the technology of "ephemeralization", doing more with less. Any technological development that tended to conserve "stocks" and reduce "flows" within the economy would be seen as a good thing. This switch would be encouraged through such measures as a tax on raw materials, a tax on power consumption and an "amortization tax" which would reach 100 per cent on products designed to last less than a year and fall to zero on products lasting 100 years or more. Briefly, there would be a shift in emphasis from quantity to quality and from the capital-intensive to the labour-intensive.

The sixth stage in the blueprint for change is a decentralization of population, industry and government bureaucracy. This is seen as a partial solution to the social problems that crop up in today's highly congested urban centres. It would also tighten relations between consumers of agricultural products and the farms on which they are produced, reducing the number of inefficient long-distance transportation links. Smaller communities would also reduce the total impact of the population on the environment, since the per-capita urban infrastructure tends to rise dramatically beyond a certain concentration of souls. Subways, expressways and large airports, for instance, are not a consideration in communities of under three or four thousand. While having "no hard and fast views" on the ideal size for the new population centres, the authors of the Blueprint tentatively recommended neighbourhoods of 500, in communities of 5,000, in nationally-represented regions of 500,000. The seventh stage on the list of programmes for change, but not necessarily the last, involved education of the populace in the necessity for the change, and in those techniques that would make it work as smoothly as possible. The authors pointed out that some of the changes they advocated would involve only a few of the seven operations listed, while in others, several of the operations might take place simultaneously.

Working from the straightforward premise that Britain should be self-supporting in food, the Blueprint set as a long-range goal the reduction of the population of the islands by 50 per cent. Its authors argued:

> Britain supports a population well in excess of the carrying capacity of the land owing to its ability to import large amounts of food, especially the cheap protein required to feed our poultry and pigs. As world population grows, and with it global agricultural demand, so will it be increasingly difficult for us to find countries with exportable surpluses which in any case will become progressively more expensive. Unless we are willing (and able) to perpetuate an even greater inequality of distribution than exists today, Britain must be self-supporting. We have stated already our belief that on the evidence available it is unlikely that there will be any significant increase in yield per acre, so that there is no other course open to us but to reduce our numbers before we stabilize. Since we appear capable of supporting no more than half our present population, the figure we should aim for over the next 150 to 200 years can be no greater than 30 million, and in order to protect it from resource fluctuation probably less.

Optimum world population, the Blueprint authors estimated, is "unlikely to be above 3.5 billion (roughly, today's figure) and is probably a good deal less". The estimate was based on three premises: that the average person needs at least 65 grams of protein a day to maintain physical and mental health, that current per-capita global agricultural production can be maintained indefinitely, and that total food supplies are distributed with absolute equality among the peoples of the world.

Responsibility for bringing national populations down to the recommended levels (or for ensuring that they do not rise above optimum numbers) would be vested in "national population services". The services would mount public education campaigns, provide free contraception, abortion and sterilization information and services, and they would commission and finance research into the subtle social determinants of population growth and new methods of contraception.

It was in regard to population control that the authors of the Blueprint may have shown a little more of their hand than they knew — specifically in recommending, without qualification, "an end to immigration" everywhere. So much for that particular freedom. And there were other, similar glimpses of a kind of chilling authoritarianism that tends to be common among those who think they have a monopoly on the truth. For example, under the heading of "Creating a new social system," the Blueprint has this to say: ". . . there is no doubt that the long transitional stage that we and our children must go through will impose a heavy burden on our moral courage and will require great restraint. Legislation and the operations of police forces and the courts will be necessary to reinforce this restraint, but we believe that such external controls can never be so subtle nor so effective as internal controls ..." And later: "As soon as the best means of inculcating the values of the stable society have been agreed upon, they should be incorporated into our educational systems. Indeed, it may not be until the generation of 40–50-year-olds have been educated in these values (so that as far as possible everybody up to the age of 50 understands them) that stable communities will achieve sufficient acceptance for them to be permanently useful."

Perhaps it was as well that the most vocal of the Blueprint's detractors contrived somehow to ignore the important issues raised by the document, including this last one, to concentrate instead on a question that had already been debated at length in both the popular press and the learned journals, and decided in favour of those once referred to as "alarmists" — the question of whether there is in fact a global environmental crisis of serious proportions. Immediately important was to define the scope of this problem as clearly and as accurately as possible, and in this the Blueprint was able to make a significant contribution — as significant, in its way, as that of *The Limits to Growth*. Maurice Strong, the energetic Canadian businessman and foreign-aid administrator who was largely responsible for bringing rich and poor nations together in Stockholm, wrote on the eve of the environment conference:

> Whatever view is taken of the seriousness of mankind's environment predicament, it is encouraging that the issues are now being discussed in public forums in many countries. One example is the debate stirred in Britain by *The Ecologist* magazine's "Blueprint for Survival", which was supported by many eminent British scientists and challenged by others, also eminent. Another is the result of the computer model developed at the Massachusetts Institute of Technology and published under the title, *The Limits to Growth*. There is no need to agree to disagree to believe that, whether or not a crisis in the very terms of human survival is on the horizon, the engagement of public concern at the overreaching issues is essential. Only in this way can a sufficient degree of political consensus be achieved — at the international level — to produce from the myriad differences of conception and opinion a programme of concerted global action.[12]

It was the struggle to obtain that consensus that gave the Stockholm conference its finest, and its bleakest, hours.

NOTES

1. Dennis L. Meadows et al., *The Limits to Growth*: London, Earth Island Press, 1972.
2. Forrester describes his model in his *World Dynamics* (Wright-Allen, 1971). His work is summarized by the present writer in *The Pollution Guide* (Toronto, Clarke Irwin, 1972).
3. Dennis Gabor, *Innovations: Scientific, Technological and Social*: Oxford University Press, 1970.
4. Other committee members included: Dr. Alison A. Anderson, U.S. (pollution); Dr. Jay M. Anderson, U.S. (pollution); Ilyas Bayar, Turkey (agriculture); Wm. W. Behrens III, U.S. (resources); Farhad Hakimzadeh, Iran (population); Dr. Steffen Harbordt, Germany (socio-political trends); Judith A. Machen, U.S. (administration); Dr. Donella H. Meadows, U.S. (population); Peter Milling, Germany (capital); Nirmala S. Murthy, India (population); Roger F. Naill, U.S. (resources); Jørgen Randers, Norway (pollution); Stephen Shantzis, U.S. (agriculture); John A. Seeger, U.S. (administration); Marlyn Williams, U.S. (documentation); Dr. Erich K. O. Zahn, Germany (agriculture).
5. The formula used to calculate the number of years world reserves of a resource will last if consumption is growing exponentially is:

$$T = \frac{\ln\,[(r \cdot s) + 1]}{r}$$

where ln = known reserves, r = average rate of growth of consumption and s = number of years reserves would last at current rate of consumption.
6. The same steady-state calculations for other resources are: chromium, 420 years; cobalt, 110; copper, 36; gold, 11; iron, 240; lead, 26; manganese, 97; mercury, 13; molybdenum, 79; natural gas, 38; nickel, 150; petroleum, 31; platinum group, 130; silver, 16; tin, 17; tungsten, 40; zinc, 23.
7. *The Limits to Growth*.
8. Early in 1972 the American Academy of Sciences, reporting on research carried out by Dr. Harold Johnston at the University of California, said: "... there appears to be general agreement that Harold Johnston's conclusion as reported in his paper 'Reduction of Stratospheric Ozone by Nitrogen Oxide Catalysts from S.S.T. Exhaust' are credible ... and that the possibility of serious effects of the normal ozone content cannot be dismissed." It is the ozone layer that protects life on earth from the harmful effects of high-frequency ultraviolet radiation from the sun.
9. Rudolf Klein, "Growth and Its Enemies": *Commentary* (Vol. 53, no. 6) June, 1972.
10. *The Ecologist* (Vol. II, no. 1) January, 1972. (Reprints are available from the magazine at Molesworth Street, Wadebridge, Cornwall, U.K. The Blueprint is also now available as a Penguin paperback.)
11. *Principles of Political Economy*, Vol. 2: London, John W. Parker, 1857. Quoted in part in "The Blueprint for Survival".
12. In *Ambio*, journal of the Royal Swedish Academy of Sciences: Vol. 1, no. 3, June, 1972.

Doomrot

Schoolchildren, on first learning about elementary statistics, sometimes project curves and conclude that they have "scientifically" predicted the future. It takes a good teacher about five minutes to show the folly of simple extrapolations. But there is a shortage of good teachers and the United Nations Conference on the Environment, which opens in Stockholm today, is likely to show it. Just audible above the grinding of political axes will be the usual silly forecasts of doom.

Compulsive extrapolators, who predict that the world is going to run out of raw materials, starve (or poison) itself to death and deprive itself of oxygen, seem to have studied neither history nor economics. One hundred years ago, these same pessimists could also have predicted imminent total calamity. Increasing pollution would choke them. Fuels like wood and coal would run out. The stench from the Thames, which sometimes made Commons committees adjourn, would spread.

In practice, much pollution has been drastically cut. The air has become much, much cleaner. The old London smogs have been ended. The Thames has been, and is still being, cleaned up. The raw materials in popular use 100 years ago have been in many instances replaced, and the process continues. The demand on coal has been cut by the invention of the internal combustion engine. Trains which are not diesel are usually electric and this power comes from generating stations which rely increasingly on oil, natural gas, and on nuclear fuel — which was scarcely thought about 30 years ago. If various metals become scarce, and thus expensive, human ingenuity replaces them with plastics. The advanced technology which makes this possible, makes it easier also to detect and prevent pollution. Governments normally monitor these matters — at least they do in capitalist countries where the polluter is not the government itself — and can take ample precautions against pollution. It would be a pity if the wilder predictions at Stockholm were merely to convince many that ecology is all bunk.

Lead editorial in the *Daily Telegraph* (London), June 5, 1972.

Chapter two

Putting it all together

If anyone still needed convincing by the summer of 1972 that there was urgent need for international discussion, and at the highest level, on the preservation of the environment, Maurice Strong offered this succinct assessment:

> Man's capacity for self-destruction is most dramatically manifested by his creating and stockpiling weapons of nuclear, chemical and biological warfare; but the environmental crisis is now making him aware of the fact that he faces a threat at least as dangerous and even more pervasive from the very processes of industrialization and urbanization that have created such unprecedented levels of wealth in the industrialized world. It confronts him with inescapable reality: that the physical world on which all human life depends consists of a complex system of relationships that is unitary in nature and global in scale; that the health of the whole system can be affected by imbalances in any part of it; and that man's own interventions in this system have reached a point where they are the principal determinants of its health.
>
> The implications are profound. For the first time in the history of man, his own activities are becoming the decisive factor in determining the future of his species. His attitudes no less than his institutions may be at an inadequate stage of evolution, but he has no choice other than to subject his activities to a degree of management unprecedented in the human experience. It is precisely this fact that gives the Stockholm conference such urgency.[1]

U Thant had been much more specific in his 1970 secretary-general's report on the environment, listing the following sample evidence as indication of the pressing need for concerted action:

> Reliance of modern technology on combustion of fossil fuels for energy has brought a ten per cent increase in atmospheric carbon dioxide over the past century. With increased rates of combustion to meet burgeoning energy demands, this could rise to 25 per cent by the year 2000. A continued increase in excess, unabsorbed carbon dioxide could have a catastrophic warming effect, melting the polar ice, changing the marine environment and creating flooding on a global scale.
>
> Modern technology has increased the amount of waste products which become pollutants. In the United States alone these wastes have included in a single year: seven million automobiles; 20 million tons of paper; 48 billion cans and 142 million tons of smoke

and noxious fumes, mostly from automobiles, power plants and factories.

All coastal nations use the sea for disposal of waste: millions of gallons of raw sewage, millions of tons of garbage dumped from barges, uncertain amounts of low-level radioactive wastes disposed of through pipelines or in sealed containers. Water used to cool power plants returns to rivers causing significant heat pollution problems.

Industries often create serious problems through pollution of air and water, damage to agricultural land and destruction of scenery. Many rivers and lakes in industrialized areas, including international waterways, are polluted by chemicals and human wastes. Fresh-water fish in some areas — even deep-sea tuna and swordfish — have been declared unfit to eat because of dangerously high levels of heavy metals.

The spread of the urban-industrial network with its associated transport facilities consumes space at a high rate. In addition, erosion and salinization have taken a toll of an estimated 500 million hectares of arable land, and two thirds of the world's forest area have been lost to production.

Some 150 species of birds and animals have become extinct due to human activities and about 1,000 species of wild animals are currently considered rare or endangered.

With the accelerating growth of the world population and rapid urbanization, more and more of the world's inhabitants live in overcrowded conditions. Wretched slums become the environment of people who once lived in greater dignity and better health on rural lands. In the developing nations, the urban population will have increased twentyfold in just 80 years between 1920 and 2000. As urban planning lags behind urban sprawl, mental distress arises from air and water pollution, inadequate transportation, congestion and noise. A number of social problems appear to be linked with overcrowding and overloading of public services: juvenile delinquency and other crime, mental breakdowns, psychosomatic illnesses, suicides, and drug addiction.

Some chemicals aiding agricultural development and health protection have adverse side effects recognized only long after they have been put in use. Pest-killing agents save crops and prevent disease, but may harm plants, wildlife, fish and the marine environment which plays an important role in maintaining atmospheric oxygen. DDT is a controversial example. An estimated billion pounds of DDT have been dumped into the environment and another 100 million pounds are added each year, although its use is now restricted in some countries.

Large-scale construction of dams, reservoirs, canals, power stations and other installations risk undesired and unplanned effects including siltation, loss of prolific delta lands, salinization, spread of water-borne disease, and displacement of people.

The U.N. had, in fact, shown an active and growing interest in environmental matters almost since its inception, even though in a specialized, compartmentalized, way. The broad sweep of U.N. economic and social efforts included many activities that were related, directly or indirectly, to the human environment: housing and community development, resource- and land-use surveys, population studies and birth-control services, schemes ranging from the Lower Mekong River Development Project to training and research programmes which it is hoped will help developing nations avoid the mistakes of the industrialized. In 1949, the organization sponsored the first Scientific Conference on the Conservation and Utilization of Resources at Lake Success. The main thrust of that conference was towards finding means to avoid the waste of precious natural resources through the application of modern technology, and expanding resource bases through discovery or creation of new resources. The need to conserve soil, forests, wildlife and fisheries was discussed, but questions of pollution, residual effects of chemicals on plant and animal life, and the ecological balance between man and other living things, were not yet recognized as matters of international concern. Five years later, in 1954, the first U.N. conference on population was held in Rome. (It predicted, incidentally, a world population of 3.5 billion by 1980: the figure had been passed by 1970.)

A number of marginally successful conventions relating to conservation of the seas and their resources had been developed through the U.N. An international convention limiting discharges of oil by ships at sea was signed in 1954, and it has been revised periodically since then. In 1958, draft conventions on the law of the sea, prepared by the International Law Commission, were approved by the first U.N. Conference on the Law of the Sea in Geneva. Three of the four conventions contained provisions relating to environmental protection, and all have been subject to periodic revision. The Convention on the High Seas which came into force in 1962 requires signatories to draw up regulations preventing marine pollution by discharge of oil from ships or pipelines, dumping of radioactive wastes, or undersea resource exploitation. The Convention on Fishing and Conservation of the Living Resources of the High Seas, coming into force in 1966, points out the need for international co-operation to avoid the danger of overfishing, and lays down rules under which conservation measures enacted by one nation may apply to others. It also establishes a procedure for the settlement of disputes by a special commission whose decisions are binding while the Convention on the Continental Shelf, which came into force in 1964, stipulates that "the exploration of the continental shelf and the exploitation of its natural resources must not result in any unjustifiable interference with navigation, fishing, or the conservation of the living resources of the sea. . ." The convention requires coastal states operating offshore installations such as oil wells to take "all appropriate measures for the protection of the living resources of the sea from harmful agents" in safety zones around them.

The U.N. Scientific Committee on the Effects of Atomic Radiation, set up in 1955, has prepared periodic reports on radioactivity levels in air, soil and bodies of water and on the effects of fallout on plant and animal life. Recent studies concern chromosomic aberrations in human cells, the effects of radiation on the human nervous system, genetic effects, and risks of malignancy. Beginning with the 1961 U.N. Conference on New Sources of Energy held in Rome, the potential uses of wind, tidal, solar and geothermal (underground steam and hot-water) energy resources have been under more intensive study. The Economic Commission for Europe (E.C.E.), a U.N.-sponsored organization taking in all European U.N. members, held its first meeting to examine the problem of water pollution in 1961, and has been increasingly active in the field since that time. In 1964, the U.N.'s Food and Agriculture Organization (F.A.O.) began a four-year project to prepare a report on conservation and the rational use of the environment. At the same time, the World Health Organization (W.H.O.) was drafting a report on world pollution problems. Both these reports were among the many examined and assessed at the ponderously-titled Intergovernmental Conference of Experts on the Scientific Basis for Rational Use and Conservation of the Resources of the Biosphere, held under U.N. auspices in Paris in September of 1968. Sixty-three nations and several specialized agencies of the U.N. attended that meeting.

In addition to this, more than twenty U.N. agencies and organizations have been involved with problems of the human environment. Some, like U.N.E.S.C.O., had been active since the U.N.'s inception. U.N.E.S.C.O.'s work has ranged from the founding, in 1948, of the International Union for the Conservation of Nature, to the launching in 1971 of a long-term intergovernmental and interdisciplinary research programme on Man and the Biosphere. Other agencies have become more active recently; the International Agency for Research on Cancer, formed in 1965, has been spending much of its time and energy on the identification and measurement of environmental carcinogens. The International Civil Aviation Agency (I.C.A.O.) has had a continuing programme of research into sonic booms and aircraft noise in the vicinity of airports. The World Meteorological Organization (W.M.O.) operates a global meteorological observation network and conducts research into inadvertent man-made climate modification. The International Atomic Energy Agency (I.A.E.A.) was charged by the U.N. parent body with establishing standards of safety to protect health and generally minimize danger to life and property from the peaceful uses of atomic energy. In 1970 the International Bank for Reconstruction and Development (often called the World Bank) announced that it had set up an office of the Environmental Advisor to ensure that projects receiving financing would "not have seriously adverse ecological consequences or, if they are likely to have such consequences that measures are taken to avoid or mitigate them." Even the General Agreement on Tariffs and Trade has been involved in environmental issues, committed as it is to ensuring that measures adopted to protect and enhance the environment are not used to buttress restrictive trading policies.

In spite of hints of poor co-ordination and wasted effort, this activity was impressive. The fact remains nonetheless that it added up to little more than monitoring research and making suggestions — except, of course, for the legal conventions; activities which amounted in the view of more than one onlooker to fighting a fire with a thermometer. Evidence was everywhere that something more was required, and required soon, in the way of international action on the environment.

Although the question of a full-dress political conference to focus the international community's attention on this need, and offer an opportunity for concrete action, had been fermenting in the minds of a number of U.N. ambassadors, it was a member of Sweden's delegation who made the formal proposal at a July, 1968 meeting of the organization's Economic and Social Council.[2] The council's resolution calling for the conference was then debated by the U.N. General Assembly. The draft document laying the ground for the Stockholm conference, although the actual site was not chosen until later, was adopted by the assembly without alteration on December 3.

As his published recollections show,[3] Sverker Aström, leader of Sweden's mission at the U.N., was far from sanguine in his answers for the question that had led him to make the gesture.

> Is the international community as it exists ... capable of action within the available time? There is hardly reason for optimism. The world is divided into sovereign states that are not willing to give up their formal freedom of action. It is one of the ironies of history that the principle of national sovereignty and equality received its triumphal confirmation in the Charter of the United

Nations at the time when the introduction of atomic weapons, the development of communications, rapid industrialization, and the awakening consciousness of environmental risks, made it unmistakably clear that all of humanity is interdependent and that the old concept of sovereignty is inadequate.

It should be remembered that the specialized agencies of the U.N. are also based on the principle of national sovereignty and are not equipped with any "supra-national" powers. They represent carefully-defined functional areas in a way that corresponds approximately to the administrative divisions within most member nations. Without strong new initiatives from their respective principals they cannot be expected to achieve the effective inter-disciplinary co-ordination of environmental endeavours that is now needed. And the governments themselves have a long way to go before they accomplish co-ordination within their own administrations.

Thus the international system as it exists today and as we must assume it will remain in the foreseeable future is inadequate and does not respond to the demands of a rapidly changing world. But if anything is to be accomplished in the international field, it must be done within this context. There is no alternative.

It was "in full recognition of this situation," Aström recalled, that Sweden promoted the conference, hoping to mobilize international awareness of the nature of the environmental crisis. "From the very beginning we emphasized the need for rapid action," Aström said. But not too rapid: Sweden, like other serious advocates of the conference, resisted pressure for an immediate meeting, holding out for 1972. The delay would put the arm on governments to take action in good time so as to show up at the conference with relatively clean noses. There was also the fact that time would be necessary for some governments to find out what the environment is.

Within a year of acceptance of the Swedish initiative by the General Assembly, it had become clear that events had to some extent overtaken planning for the conference. Under the 1968 resolution, the main thrust of the meeting was to have been "to provide a framework for comprehensive consideration within the U.N. of the problems of the human environment in order to focus the attention of governments and public opinion on the importance and urgency of this question."[4] But by the time of the next assembly session 12 months later it had become clear that public feeling — at least in the developed world — had already been inflamed to the point where concern was growing over a predicted backlash of conservative opinion. The massive international "Earth Day" teach-ins and demonstrations had come and gone, journalistic exposes were legion, and "eco-freaks" abounded. Public pressure for action was enormous, and still intensifying. Throughout most of the industrialized world, just as it had once been impossible to deliver a political speech without referring to God, it was now unthinkable to neglect a mention of ecology. With this in mind the assembly effected a shift in the direction of the conference, giving a second and overriding purpose "to serve as a practical means to encourage and to provide guidelines for action by governments and international organizations".[5]

The herculean job of preparing for what was to become perhaps the best-documented, best-organized conference ever held by the U.N., was put in the hands of a 27-member preparatory committee with strong representation from the third world. Between March, 1970 and the same month in 1972, the committee held four two-week meetings in New York and Geneva. To supplement these discussions, a series of regional seminars was held in Addis Ababa, Bangkok, Mexico City and Beirut. Meanwhile, background documentation began piling up in the form of special reports from the many U.N. agencies concerned with environmental matters, and from intergovernmental organizations, national state-of-the-environment reports case studies from nearly 90 different countries, together with papers from non-governmental organizations ranging from the Boy Scouts to the World Wildlife Fund. The eventual total was well over one hundred thousand pages.

Preparations were still in their preliminary stages and lagging badly when, on December 7, 1970, the General Assembly confirmed Maurice Strong's appointment as secretary-general to the conference. His enormous personal energy soon had work moving ahead at full speed. Strong, a spare man with a modest civil-service moustache and a perpetually startled look about him, was born in 1929, the son of an impoverished assistant Canadian Pacific Railway station agent in Oak Lake, Manitoba. A victim of the Depression, Strong's father was unemployed during most of his son's boyhood, and the family, enlarged by three younger children, moved from one threadbare dwelling to another, often scraping hard for the rent money. The poverty of those years, which ruined his mother's health and was eased only as his father enlisted in the R.C.A.F. at the outbreak of war, gave a radicalism to Strong's thinking that was to remain with him in maturity. As he recalled in a pre-conference interview with the *New Yorker*:

> I kept thinking, what kind of society is this, when it takes a war that's killing people to save my father's life by giving him a job? ... I didn't believe that what was happening to poor people was right and I still don't. ... One's whole life is clearly shaped by early actions and my life has been clearly shaped by the ambitions

and drives I developed early. Because of my experience, I feel that the elimination of basic poverty should be man's top priority. The existence of mass poverty is totally incompatible with the concept of human dignity. It was my long-standing concern with the destructiveness of poverty that got me into foreign-aid work; two thirds of the population of the earth are really afflicted by poverty, and I felt I could make an impact there. In handling foreign aid, I became increasingly aware of the importance of interdependence on earth, and that — not merely pollution — is at the heart of the environment issue: the necessity of conducting ourselves on this planet in a way that corresponds with the realities of the physical world. To survive, we simply must have better standards of collaborative behaviour. Rugged individualism is passé. A high-technology civilization like ours inherently requires more co-operative attitudes. We live in apartments and shop in super-markets and are utterly interdependent, but we still tend to behave all too often as though we were blazing trails through forests. Now, I'm not for world government and I'm not for uniformity; I think that the strongest political and ecological systems are those that preserve variety. But you can't let variety run rampant. The environmental issue is more a matter of political and social management than anything else. You can't go on forever with four competing service stations at every crossroads and a deficiency of hospital beds.

Strong had completed high school by the time he was 15, but while in Winnipeg to enrol for courses at the University of Manitoba he applied for a job instead, as an apprentice fur trader with the Hudson's Bay Company, and was accepted. Shipped off by the company to Chesterfield Inlet in the North-West Territories, he shelved his university career permanently, as things developed, although by early 1972 he had received ten honorary degrees. Spending just a year with the Bay, Strong used his time profitably, learning the Eskimo language and studying the economics texts he had lugged north. At 17, he formed a mining exploration company with a northern prospector, but soon dropped that in favour of work with the newly-formed United Nations, which hired him in 1947 as an assistant pass officer, a job involving supervision of a corps of messengers at temporary U.N. headquarters in Lake Placid, N.Y. With characteristic certainty he decided then that his future lay with the fledgling international organization. Lack of a university degree barred him from promotion, however, and after a brief stint with the R.C.A.F. as a pilot trainee (he was washed out for poor depth perception) he moved to Calgary to take up a position as a mining and oil stock analyst with a brokerage house. In 1951 he became assistant general manager of Dome Petroleum only to decide, on the spur of the moment, to sell his house and furniture and devote two years to seeing the world with his wife, whom he had married only a few months earlier. Much of their time was spent in Africa: in Nairobi, Strong learned to speak Swahili while Mau Mau uprisings were setting the country aflame.

Returning to Canada at 25, he tried to find a job with several different international development agencies, but was turned down once again for his lack of a university degree. It was thus that Strong returned to Calgary and Dome Petroleum, soon to become the company's vice-president. By the age of 30, he was running his own consultative firm as well as an oil company called Canadian International Gas and Oil. Three years later, in 1962, he was hired to head the giant Power Corporation of Canada, a position that carried with it directorships of 30 other Canadian and American companies. In 1965, the late Prime Minister Lester Pearson asked Strong to take over as director-general of Canada's external aid office, later renamed the Canadian International Development Agency (C.I.D.A.). He accepted the job, though it meant a salary cut of $163,000 a year. Plunging into his work with typical zest, he had proved himself so valuable an asset within four years that Prime Minister Pierre Trudeau at first refused when U Thant asked for Strong's release to take charge of planning for the Stockholm conference. Only after earnest representations from Aström and Swedish Prime Minister Olaf Palme did Trudeau reluctantly accede to Thant's request.

Strong brought with him to the job of conference secretary-general an easy balance of virtues: coming from a developed nation, he nonetheless understood the problems and needs of the developing world; with organizational and administrative abilities well proven in one of the more hectic areas of business, his work with the developing nations had at the same time developed in him a commitment to the kind of global co-operation and social justice the U.N. symbolized. Moreover he was quietly — one might say inoffensively — Canadian. His first decision on taking the U.N. job was to be one of his most important: he dispatched Chester Ronning, a seasoned Canadian diplomatic troubleshooter, to Peking, to convince Premier Chou En-lai that China should attend the conference. Influenced in no small measure by Strong's personal integrity and commitment (and perhaps by the fact that he could claim a distant relationship to the late Anna Louisa Strong, an American left-wing journalist and friend of the Chinese revolution), the Chinese accepted the invitation, thereby immediately and immeasurably bolstering the prestige of the Stockholm gathering.

Strong noted early in the planning process that no satisfactory definition had been arrived at for "human environment", and so formulated
his own: "The term 'human environment' refers to those aspects of
man's activities which, by affecting the natural ecological systems of
which he is part, affect his own life and well being." It was not a classic
exegesis, but it worked. Next, the conference was broken down into
three more easily-manageable abstract levels. Level I was to be the
intellectual-conceptual level, and would include a "distinguished lecture series", to run concurrently with conference proceedings amid the
baroque splendour of the mirror ballroom of the venerable Grand
Hotel. Speakers were to include Thor Heyerdahl, Sir Solly Zuckerman,
Aurelio Peccei, Georges Baranescu, Gunnar Myrdal, Lady Barbara
Ward Jackson and René Dubos. Also included under the Level I
heading was the preparation of a "report on the human environment"
written by Lady Jackson (better known to students of economic philosophy as Barbara Ward) and Dubos, the biologist and environmentalist,
in consultation with a panel of scientific and intellectual leaders from
58 countries. Not an official document, the book was intended to set the
stage and establish a mood for the conference. It was published in
several languages under the title, *Only One Earth*. The London *Times*
review by Wayland Kennet was typical of the welcome it received:
"The appearance of *Only One Earth* is an event to be celebrated. One
can hardly imagine more difficult circumstances for the creation of a
good book. It was commissioned not free-born, written to a very short
deadline, had two authors, and was commented on by no fewer than
seventy eminent and idiosyncratic consultants. That a book with that
history should be any good at all is surprising: that it should be, as it is,
a very good book indeed, is almost miraculous. . . . The scared will be
reassured by it, and the complacent shaken. . . . The Stockholm conference is the world's work and *Only One Earth* is fully worthy to be
its work book." The book was above all a reflection of the imposing
intelligence and vigour of Lady Jackson. Level I also encompassed the
grandly-conceived but somewhat less splendidly-executed Declaration
on the Human Environment, which was to be a comprehensive affir-
mation of the human right to a livable world (Appendix 2).

Level II was to be the "action plan" level, and include all the many
recommendations that would arise out of the conference for national
and international action in various fields. It was to be the first comprehensive response by the international community to the questions:
what are the principal challenges and opportunities facing man with
regard to protecting and enhancing his environment? What gaps in

knowledge must be filled to enable a response to those challenges and opportunities? What people and institutions are needed at the local, regional and global levels to fill those knowledge gaps? What are the measures that should be taken to harmonize development goals and social and cultural values with environmental quality objectives?

Level III, the "action completed" level, would take in any measures which could reasonably be hoped to be dealt with and completed during the conference — for example, the setting up and funding of a U.N. environmental agency. The actual work of the conference was to be undertaken in plenary meetings and in three committees of the whole, and would consist for the most part of examination, amendment and approval or rejection of recommendations drafted by the preparatory commission in six main subject areas: planning and management of human settlements for environmental quality; environmental aspects of natural-resources management; identification and control of pollutants of broad international significance; educational, informational, social and cultural aspects of environmental issues; development and the environment, and implications of action proposals in terms of international organization.

Conference preparations were moving smoothly into their final stages when that dinosaur of a world problem — the cold-war dispute over the fate of divided Germany — with a swipe of its tail knocked a dangerous number of props out from under the conference structure. The shock came a short five months before the discussions were to open, with the Soviet Union's announcement that it would not take part in the final meeting of the preparatory commission, a body to which it had until then been making a weighty and constructive contribution. Worse than that, the Russians also stated their intention to boycott the conference itself, which meant that their east European allies Poland, Bulgaria, Hungary, and Czechoslovakia would also be staying away. For a few confused and jittery days it seemed possible that Russia had pulled the rug out from under the whole plan.

What the Russians were protesting was the Christmas decision by the U.N.'s General Assembly to limit attendance at Stockholm to those nations that were members either of the U.N. or one or more of its specialized agencies. The move took the form of a vote by 104 with nine against and seven abstentions, to base full participation in the conference on the 26-year-old "Vienna formula", a standard piece of U.N. protocol. The motion had been proposed jointly by Great Britain and the U.S. It meant that West Germany, as a member of U.N.E.S.C.O. and W.H.O., could attend, but East Germany could not.

Delicate east-west negotiations were launched almost immediately for a compromise formula by which East Germany could participate, but they were hampered seriously by events unfolding elsewhere in the realm of international politics. By late 1971, after years of heart-breakingly difficult negotiation first as foreign minister and then as chancellor of the West German republic, Willy Brandt was finally within sight of the ultimate goal of his *Ostpolitik*. The long-awaited normalization of relations between West Germany and the eastern bloc, including East Germany, had been successfully negotiated in two re-lated friendship treaties, one with the Soviet Union and the other with Poland. And awaiting final approval of these agreements by Bonn was a British-French-American-Soviet accord which would make the normal-ization complete and workable, granting East Germany full political recognition. A major result would be freer contact between the two halves of Germany and across the Berlin wall, with all that meant to a people divided for 25 years, and to the rest of a world that had been kept perpetually on the edge of its seat by the resulting frictions.

As the date for ratification of the two friendship pacts by the West German Bundestag grew closer, however, what support there had been within Bonn's parliamentary opposition began to crumble. With only a razor-thin majority, Brandt had pinned his hopes on the apparently overwhelming public support for the treaties to force opposition parties to allow their passage. For nearly three weeks previously, in fact, opposition leader Rainer Barzel had been trying to work out a bi-partisan approach. The outcome was in doubt until the last possible moment. At 11 o'clock on the morning of the vote, Barzel finally gave up trying to persuade his Christian-Democratic Union deputies and their Bavarian allies to take heed of public opinion and vote for the treaties along with a covering all-party resolution confirming ties with the West. Instead he joined the growing ranks of conservatives, grouped around Bavarian Party leader Franz Josef Strauss, demanding unan-imous abstention from voting. At 3 p.m. on May 17, 1972, when the 496-member *Bundestag* assembled, it was still unclear whether absten-tions and negative votes would rob the West German chancellor of the simple majority he needed. Polling began. On the treaty with Moscow, the opposition put up 238 abstentions and nine noes, leaving Brandt with a two-vote whisper of a majority. A half-hour later the Warsaw treaty scraped through by the same slim margin. It was with the ex-quisite delicacy of this situation in mind that Brandt's coalition govern-ment had taken part in the negotiations to find a way out of the impasse that looked like keeping the east bloc away from Stockholm. His most cherished political dreams — and indeed, his political future — at stake, it is difficult in retrospect to blame Brandt for insisting that no concession be made which might topple the finely-balanced majority he was struggling to hold together for the historic treaty votes.

During the east-west talks a compromise acceptable to the West Germans was in fact worked out. It would have given East Germany complete working participation in the conference, excluding the right to vote. But a New York *Times* story revealing the compromise so incensed the east Europeans that they broke off the talks. Further attempts to rebuild an understanding proved fruitless. Bonn's passage of the two treaties once again raised a remote hope, however, that the Soviet Union and her allies might yet turn up in Stockholm. Last-minute preparations were made on the assumption that they would appear: 30 of the fleet of hundreds of freshly-minted robin's-egg-blue Volvos and Saabs supplied to delegations were set aside, 220 hotel beds were kept open, and the proper documents distributed. It was even agreed to leave one of the vice-chairmanships open for the first day or two of the conference, in the hope that it might be filled by a Soviet delegate as custom and protocol normally dictated.

In the end, of course, the Russians did stay away, as did the Poles, Hungarians, and Czechoslovaks. It was one of history's ironic coincidences that on the day the conference was officially opened by U.N. Secretary-General Kurt Waldheim — June 4, 1972 — evening newscasts announced the signing in Berlin of the Big Four accord that paved the way for East Germany's entry into the U.N. simultaneously with West Germany, granted western recognition of the East German regime after 23 years of diplomatic ostracism, and normalized relations between the two Germanies.

As the 114 states that did attend[6] got down to the business at hand, however, the eastern boycott came to be seen in a more realistic perspective. The Russians and their allies had, after all, participated actively in planning the conference until the end, and the documents which would be considered at Stockholm bore their unmistakable imprint. Furthermore they would have their opportunity to comment on the work of the conference, and press for any revisions or alterations they thought important, when the Stockholm proceedings were presented to the General Assembly for final approval. The absence of the east Europeans in no way indicated a lack of commitment to finding solutions to the crisis in the environment. It was due rather to an unrelated political dispute that was anyway all but settled. Their failure to attend, however regrettable, was by no means disastrous.

NOTES

1. *Ambio*, June, 1972.
2. Credit for originally conceiving the idea of a U.N. conference on environmental questions has been variously given to Barbara Ward (Lady Jackson) and to former U.N. employee, and now Swedish foreign-office environment specialist, Inga Thorsson.
3. *Ambio*, February, 1972.
4. General Assembly resolution 2398 (XXIII), Dec. 3, 1968.
5. General Assembly resolution 2581 (XXIV), Dec. 15, 1969.
6. Representatives of the following 114 states invited in accordance with General Assembly resolution 2850 (XXVI) took part in the conference: Afghanistan, Algeria, Argentina, Australia, Austria, Bahrein, Bangladesh, Belgium, Bolivia, Botswana, Brazil, Burundi, Cameroun, Canada, Central African Republic, Ceylon, Chad, Chile, China, Colombia, Congo, Costa Rica, Cyprus, Dahomey, Denmark, Dominican Republic, Ecuador, Egypt, El Salvador, Ethiopia, Federal Republic of Germany, Fiji, Finland, France, Gabon, Ghana, Greece, Guatemala, Guinea, Guyana, Haiti, Holy See, Honduras, Iceland, India, Indonesia, Iran, Iraq, Ireland, Israel, Italy, Ivory Coast, Jamaica, Japan, Jordan, Kenya, Kuwait, Lebanon, Lesotho, Liberia, Libyan Arab Republic, Liechtenstein, Luxembourg, Madagascar, Malawi, Malaysia, Malta, Mauritania, Mauritius, Mexico, Monaco, Morocco, Nepal, Netherlands, New Zealand, Nicaragua, Niger, Nigeria, Norway, Pakistan, Panama, Peru, Philippines, Portugal, Republic of Korea, Republic of Viet-Nam, Romania, San Marino, Senegal, Singapore, South Africa, Spain, Sudan, Swaziland, Sweden, Switzerland, Syrian Arab Republic, Thailand, Togo, Trinidad and Tobago, Tunisia, Turkey, Uganda, United Arab Emirates, United Kingdom of Great Britain and Northern Ireland, United Republic of Tanzania, United States of America, Upper Volta, Uruguay, Venezuela, Yemen, Yugoslavia, Zaire, Zambia.

    The Secretary-General of the United Nations attended the conference. The conference was attended also by representatives of the Secretary-General from the department of Economic and Social Affairs, the regional economic commissions, the United Nations Economic and Social Office in Beirut, the United Nations Conference on Trade and Development, and the United Nations Industrial Development Organization.

    The following specialized agencies were represented: International Labour Organization, Food and Agriculture Organization, United Nations Educational Scientific and Cultural Organization, World Health Organization, International Bank for Reconstruction and Development, International Monetary Fund, Universal Postal Union, International Telecommunication Union, World Meteorological Organization, and Intergovernmental Maritime Consultative Organization. The International Atomic Energy Agency and the General Agreement on Tariffs and Trade were also represented.

Concorde Manoeuvres

STOCKHOLM — *Britain and France have taken a joint initiative through confidential diplomatic channels in an effort to prevent the Concorde supersonic jet becoming a major item on the agenda at the United Nations environment conference here next week. The two countries' ambassadors in the Swedish capital, Sir Guy Millard and M. Pierre Francsort, obtained an appointment at the Swedish foreign ministry two weeks ago, where they told a senior official that it was desirable that the U.N. meeting "should not reach premature conclusions that the Concorde would be harmful to the environment".*

It was not clear if the two ambassadors were demanding outright that Sweden, as the host country, should try to keep any mention of Concorde off the agenda altogether. If so, they were treading on thin ice, because Sweden, together with Norway and Denmark, is determined to raise the issue of whether supersonic commercial airliners are a grave threat to the atmosphere. The Scandinavian countries have banned supersonic flights over their territories. One thing that is bound to arouse antagonism among other delegations is the very fact that Britain and France attempted this piece of secret diplomacy rather than being candid about their stand. The Swedes may have decided to leak the affair now, close to the opening of the conference itself, or the facts may simply have come out inadvertently through conference sources.

Belated confirmation of the initiative last night by Whitehall and the Quai d'Orsay, can only result in raising suspicions at Stockholm when the conference opens on Monday, that the two rich western industrial nations are out to achieve something by stealth. This hardly makes for a smooth run for the conference.

The Guardian, June 2, 1972.

Chapter three

The poor nations state their case

Strong was careful to leave no stone unturned in his attempt to minimize the impact of the Russian boycott. On the opening day of the
conference, hectic negotiations were undertaken to bring the East Germans to Stockholm in the capacity of "experts", a device which had
previously allowed that nation to attend W.H.O. gatherings. When
these failed to bear fruit, Strong turned to a device that would at least
make it difficult for the Russians to behave in future as if the conference had not taken place — it was a well-kept secret that in Stockholm he met Russian embassy officials each day to brief them on
conference proceedings.

If the eastern bloc's absence was a cause for worry, the large turnout
of nations from the developing world was a source of no small amount
of relief. There had been a time, early in the planning stages of the
conference, when it appeared the third-world nations would be staying
away in droves. When the proposal for an environment conference was
first broached, opinion among the developing nations ranged from an
assumption that problems relating to the environment were a concern
for the highly-developed nations alone — the side effects of a high
per-capita G.N.P. — to a belief that the developed nations were using
environmental doomsday predictions as a racist device to keep the non-
white third world at a relatively low level of development. Environmental concerns were a neat excuse for the industrialized nations to
pull the ladder up behind them.

From the beginning, Strong and the conference secretariat con-
centrated much of their effort on dispelling these suspicions and
encouraging third-world nations to take an active interest in the conference. Some developed nations, notably Canada, participated, des-
patching consultants to developing nations to help with the drafting of
the national environmental reports and case histories requested by the
conference secretariat. In his personal campaign to soften the attitudes
of the developing nations, Strong was to travel hundreds of thousands
of miles over every continent except Antarctica in the months preceding the conference. He personally guaranteed scores of African and
Asian leaders that their interests would be respected. January and
February in 1972 were typical months: he visited Brazil for talks with

that nation's president; he travelled to Jamaica to survey the island's environmental problems, and from there flew to Stockholm to meet with the Swedish preparatory committee. Then it was off to attend an Arab League Cultural and Scientific Organization seminar in Khartoum, followed by trips to Egypt, Jordan, Syria, Iraq and Kuwait.

By April of 1972, Strong was able to say in an interview:[1] "I think, in fact, one of the major objectives of the Stockholm conference has already been accomplished, in that it has made people aware of how interdependent the world is, both developed and underdeveloped. ... What we have done is to put the environmental issue in front of them [the developing nations]. When they see an issue like this, they react, they see its importance. They are deeply committed, much more so than even a year ago." There were two principal reasons for this change in atmosphere, and Strong's personal resourcefulness was openly acknowledged as one of them by delegation leaders at Stockholm. "Frankly, when preparations for this conference started in earnest barely two years ago," stated Professor Adebayo Adedeji, Nigeria's Federal Commissioner for Economic Development and Reconstruction, "most people at the governmental level in Nigeria were inclined to be skeptical about the objectives and the motives of the force behind its organization. The concern of the industrialized nations with measures to curb pollution appeared to us as yet another obstacle in the already handicapped race for material progress. Mr. Strong, through the sincerity of his advocacy, soon made it clear that all of us, irrespective of the stage of our development, have a large stake in the matter. I am proud to say that my country thereafter played its part in the preparatory work of this conference and we remain fully committed to the search for a way out of the human predicament ..."

A second motive for growing commitment on the part of the developing nations stemmed from the conference secretariat's early decision to convene a panel of third-world scientists and development experts at Founex, Switzerland, on June 4-12, 1971, and to follow this up later in the same year with the already-mentioned regional meetings of the U.N. Economic Commission for Asia and the Far East (E.C.A.F.E.) in Bangkok (August 17-23), the U.N. Economic Commission for Africa (E.C.A.) in Addis Ababa (August 23-27), the U.N. Economic Commission for Latin America (E.C.L.A.) in Mexico City (September 6-11), and the U.N. Economic and Social Office in Beirut (U.N.E.S.O.B.) from September 27 to October 2. The Founex report became one of the conference's most important documents and was attached to the conference working paper on subject area V, development and environment. Its first few paragraphs offer a lucid outline of the position taken by most developing countries:

> The current concern with the human environment has arisen at a time when the energies and efforts of the developing countries are being increasingly devoted to the goal of development. Indeed, the compelling urgency of the development objective has been widely recognized in the last two decades by the international community and has more recently been endorsed in the proposals set out by the United Nations for the Second Development Decade.
>
> To a large extent, the current concern with environmental issues has emerged out of the problems experienced by the industrially advanced countries. These problems are themselves very largely the outcome of a high level of economic development. The creation of large productive capacities in industry and agriculture, the growth of complex systems of transportation and communication, the evolution of massive urban conglomerations, have all been accompanied in one way or another by damage and disruption to the human environment. ... The developing countries are not, of course, unconcerned with these problems. They have an obvious and a vital stake in them to the extent of their impact on the global environment and on their economic relations with the developed countries. They also have an interest in them to the extent that they are problems that tend to accompany the process of development and are in fact already beginning to emerge, with increasing severity, in their own societies. The developing countries would clearly wish to avoid, as far as is feasible, the mistakes and distortions that have characterized the patterns of development of the industrialized societies.
>
> However, the major environmental problems of developing countries are essentially of a different kind. They are predominantly problems that reflect the poverty and very lack of development of their societies. They are problems, in other words, of both rural and urban poverty. In both the towns and the countryside, not merely the "quality of life", but all life itself is endangered by poor water, housing, sanitation and nutrition, by sickness and disease and by natural disasters. These are problems, no less than those of industrial pollution, that clamour for attention in the context of the concern with human environment. They are problems which affect the greater mass of mankind.
>
> It is evident that, in large measure, the kind of environmental problems that are of importance in developing countries are those that can be overcome by the process of development itself. In advanced countries, it is appropriate to view development as a cause of environmental problems. Badly planned and unregulated development can have a similar result in developing countries as well. But, for the greater part, developing countries must view the relationship between development and environment in a different

perspective. In their context, development becomes essentially a cure for their major environmental problems.

The attitudes thus expressed were reinforced, often in the bluntest of terms, as the developing nations took their turns at the *Folkets Hus* podium during the plenary debate. The Ivory Coast announced that it would like to have more pollution problems, "in so far as they are evidence of industrialization". Not only was the idea that growth and pollution are necessarily related "false and pernicious", but in fact only industrial growth was capable of overcoming the population problem. The Libyan delegation affirmed that "the big states are responsible for the destruction, spoliation and pollution that deteriorated [*sic*] the human environment. These states cannot avoid their obligation and duties." Libya's point, that the developing nations were facing costs resulting from pollution generated by an industrial complex whose benefits they did not enjoy, was one the industrialized nations tried hard to ignore — without, as it developed, much success.

The report went on to express some of the developing nations' more pressing fears with regard to the new environmental concerns: "Environmental issues," it stated,

> may come to exercise a growing influence on international economic relations. They are not only a formidable competitor for developed countries' resources (which in some instances might have been channelled towards development assistance), but they are also a factor which, to an ever-increasing degree, could influence the pattern of world trade, the international distribution of industry, the competitive position of different groups of countries, their comparative costs of production, etc. Environmental actions by developed countries may have a profound and many-fold impact on the growth and external economic relations of developing countries.

More specifically, the report continued,

> some environmental actions by developed countries (restrictions on the import of certain commodities, imposition of environmental regulations, standards and other non-tariff barriers on imports as well as increased production costs reflected in higher export prices) are likely to have a negative effect on the developing countries' export possibilities and their terms of trade. Recycling of raw materials may also tend to diminish the volume of primary commodities consumed and imported into developed countries.

With typical candour and disdain for the diplomatic niceties so well refined by the older European states over the centuries, the developing nations — particularly the African ex-colonial countries — insisted on hauling the skeletons of colonialism, imperialism and racism out of the closet and displaying them for everyone to see. "As for the racist govern-ment of South Africa and other agents of colonial oppression like the Portuguese," Nigeria's impeccable Professor Adedeji averred in omi-nous tones, "their presence here deceives no one. They cannot treat the environment with concern and consideration if they treat the vast majority of mankind inhabiting the countries which they dominate with less than human consideration. We cannot get through to an appropriate management of resources in the interest of humanity if in our daily acts and daily pronouncements some of us show that human beings themselves mean nothing." And this from the Libyan delegation, who chose to run the whole gamut of issues in a speech that was a sincere symphony of malapropisms:

> The Libyan Arab Republic, which believe deeply that it is "Only One Earth" as a means to protect natural environment to protect human life as a target in itself requests that this conference should not put aside what is occurring on this earth of persecution, unjustice and oppression. This conference has to face its historical responsibilities and cannot ignore that a whole nation has been expelled from its historical land and its heritage, its present and future destroyed and turned into refugees as Palestinian people. And cannot ignore preventing people from their rights in free life on their lands. It also cannot ignore domination of minorities on people's abilities and destinies that is happening in several areas of Africa where, as well as in the U.S.A., people are still suffering from racial segregation [and] discrimination. It also cannot ignore destruction of [the] human environment in Indochina by biological warfare and modern equipment and incineration materials. The conference, besides, cannot ignore mass destruction, spoiling lands and crops, environmental pollution by human bodies who are unfairly killed, nor mass murders of moslems minority in [the] Philippines, all these aspects and events put the historical and human responsibilities on the conference to face the reality that "Man" is subject to extermination besides what is caused to his environment of destruction and corruption.

Colombia, painfully aware like the rest of the under-developed world of the fact that the 20 per cent of the world's population enjoying the fruits of advanced development was using up 80 per cent of the world's resources, commented bitterly on the "merciless" exploitation of the developing nations' heritage. The developed nations, because they were first in, enjoyed the immense benefits of getting all the most accessible and most easily exploitable resources. As Ward and Dubos pointed out in *Only One Earth*, nearly all the manganese was removed from areas like Ghana at no more cost than the subsistence wages paid to the

"natives". Millions of tons of oil similarly left the Middle East at rock-
bottom prices before post-war nationalism in the area forced a more
equitable sharing of profits. Dr. W. K. Chagul, Minister of Economic
Affairs and Development Planning for Tanzania, got down to specific
cases:

> The evils of *apartheid,* racial and colonial oppression, far from
> being irrelevant, are at the very core of environmental problems
> in Africa due to the degradation they cause to the human resources
> by taking away the rights of the many and thereby bringing bene-
> fits to only a minority. It is in this vein that Tanzania expects the
> conference to take a definite stand against such projects as the
> Cabora Bassa and the proposed Kunene dams whose purpose is to
> perpetuate a system of human degradation, discrimination and of
> colonial domination. The evil intent of these projects was noted by
> the 26th U.N. General Assembly which condemned "their con-
> struction as designed to entrench and further colonialist and
> racialist domination over the territories of Southern Africa and
> which were a source of international tension". As these projects
> envisage the displacement of the indigenous people by the settling
> of foreigners, they are indeed at the very heart of the debasement
> of man and his environment . . .

The hydro-electric dams referred to by the minister were also the
subject of an urgent communique delivered by Zambia to Strong in
Geneva a year earlier. It is a case that helps explain how the perennial
frustrations felt by many of the third-world nations had helped shape
their particular viewpoint on environmental issues. Both dams are
being built in the heart of a southern Africa peopled in large measure
by newly and proudly independent black Africans. Both are being
financed jointly by South Africa and Portugal and are designed prin-
cipally to benefit those nations and their dependencies. The Cabora
Bassa, on the Zambezi in Portuguese Mozambique near where Zambia,
Malawi, and Rhodesia meet, would be 70 per cent bigger than the
Aswan project in Egypt and have an environmental impact within a
radius of 1,200 miles. The equally ambitious Kunene dam is to be
placed on the river of the same name that has its source in central
Angola and empties into the South Atlantic near the desert areas of
Namibia. The total power generated by the two dams would be in the
neighbourhood of 3,850 megawatts. The Kunene project alone would
permit irrigation of some 500,000 hectares of dry land. Zambia argued
that

> South Africa, which is also using forced labour, further [aside from
> the obvious benefits of energy] needs these two schemes to enforce

its racialist theory of a "Third Africa" based on a minority regime, with the Portuguese administration playing a secondary role in its colonies in a desperate attempt to maintain its presence there. . . . Both Cabora Bassa and Kunene projects are being made very much against the wishes of local populations, of immediately neighbouring countries like Zambia and Tanzania and of other African countries. The problem here becomes a more burning issue, as both . . . projects call for the installation of foreign white settlers in Mozambique and Angola — a process which has already started.

Turning to questions more directly related to the ostensible subject area of the Stockholm conference, the communique went on to demand that all of the nations likely to be affected by the projects be involved in the planning and operation of them — an argument difficult to deny but at the same time largely unacceptable to South Africa and Portugal. "If errors made in the developed continents of Europe and North America are to be avoided, both Cabora Bassa and Kunene projects must be first submitted to as meticulous examination from an ecological viewpoint as is being done in our world today in the nuclear, ballistic or astronautic fields. It would be fatally wrong to believe that ecology is a less serious matter," the note concluded.

After long years of waiting for the independence that would give them essential power over the exploitation of their natural resources and the direction of their development, ex-colonial nations in southern Africa were finding that they still lacked control over their economic or environmental destinies. Several of the nations of Latin America were to argue in a similar way that the "economic imperialism" of multi-national corporations, based in the U.S. and elsewhere, was depriving them of effective control of their economies, and resulting in the rapaciously wasteful spoliation of their resource bases, carried out under absentee managers who had no real concern for the local environment. Any efforts to control such policies of foreign-owned corporations, they complained, were seriously hampered by the lack of scientific and engineering expertise needed to formulate and enforce environmental guidelines.

The issue of "consultation" implicit in these arguments emerged as one of the most contentious topics in the conference. A bitter quarrel between Brazil and Argentina over the former's plan to construct a dam on a river, the Pirana, that has its source in Brazil but empties into the sea by Argentinian territory, was directly relevant. Something of a *bête noire* at Stockholm, Brazil's speech to the plenary contained the following dubious observations. More research should be undertaken before environmental action is contemplated. Economic development must be

viewed as a compromise between raising standards of living and lower-
ing the quality of the environment. Developing nations cannot afford
to spend money on environmental protection (and so the argument that
they cannot afford not to is false). Pollution problems in developing
nations tend to be strictly internal ones and some, such as sewage, are
taken care of by natural processes. One should be confident that solutions to the world's environmental ills will be found in time — views to
the contrary are "exaggerated and highly emotional". There is no truth
to the rumour that some natural resources are in short supply. The
present situation is actually one of oversupply and insufficient demand,
and experience has shown that scarcity always leads to discovery of new
supplies. The concept of national sovereignty must in no way be diluted
by any U.N. agreements relating to the environment. A high rate of
economic growth is essential for continuance of environmental protection policies.

When to these statements was added the fact that Brazil's expansion
into its vast interior is taking a course hardly less predatory, genocidal,
and generally ill-advised than that of 19th-century America, it came as
no surprise that the country should deny Argentina's right to be con-
sulted on the plans for damming the international river. While officially
deploring the "destructive" bickering between the two nations, many a
"more reasonable" state showed keen private concern, for what continental country did not share some of its rivers and lakes with border-
ing states? Certainly not the U.S., or any of the European nations
flanking the Rhine.

The conference working paper that dealt most directly with the
question of consultation was the draft Declaration on the Human
Environment (Appendix 2). Principle 20 of the draft read: "Relevant
information must be supplied by states on activities or developments
within their jurisdiction or under their control whenever they believe,
or have reason to believe, that such information is needed to avoid the
risk of significant adverse effects on the environment in areas beyond
their national jurisdiction." The issue, therefore, had to be resolved one
way or the other in the ad-hoc committee set up at the suggestion of
China to examine the draft. During that group's deliberations (examined in detail in Chapter 5) more than one issue raised by the awe-
somely potent Chinese delegation — issues no less contentious on the
surface than that of consultation — was resolved satisfactorily. Strangely,
however, the committee was "unable" to arrive at any solution to principle 20, the only vocal objector to which was Brazil. Clearly, there was

simply not the will on the part of a number of states — notably the U.S.[2] and western European nations — to go out of their way to commit themselves to this elementary principle. The ambiguous position of these countries twisted itself into a series of inexplicable, rosily favourable comments on the "brilliance" and "hard-working" nature of the Brazilian delegation which were to be a source of continual bafflement for reporters attending press conferences and briefings held by these delegations. The guilt that spawned this disingenuous praise was visible only in retrospect. Principle 20 was to be the only section of the Declaration on the Human Environment tabled and left for debate in the next meeting of the U.N. General Assembly.

A second key area of concern for the developing nations at the conference surrounded what came to be known as the "compensation" issue, the question of whether nations whose exports were hurt by imposition of strict environmental-protection standards by importing countries should get compensation for their losses. A case in point might be the refusal of France to accept delivery of a shipment of foodstuffs from Algeria because pesticide residue levels exceeded French standards. Also involved in this issue was the whole question of environmental standards being used as a covert kind of trade barrier. The developing nations, already suffering from what they felt were unfair trade patterns, imposed by the rich industrialized countries to protect their position of relative affluence, were naturally anxious to see that this did not occur. The debate was long and thorny, and it took place in committee three, charged with examining the subject area of development and the environment. Principle 32 of the working paper dealing with this topic provided the focus for the discussion, stating the case clearly:

> In order to ensure that the growing concern with the environment does not lead to major disruptions in international trade, it is recommended that governments take the necessary steps to ensure that: — all countries present at the conference agree not to invoke environmental concerns as a pretext for discriminatory trade policies or for reduced access to markets and recognize further that the burdens of the environmental policies of the industrialized countries should not be transferred, either directly or indirectly, to the developing countries; — where environmental concerns lead to restrictions on trade, or to stricter environmental standards with negative effects on exports, particularly from developing countries, appropriate measures for compensation should be worked out; — the G.A.T.T. (General Agreement on Tariffs and Trade) could be

used for the examination of the problems, specifically through the recently established Group on Environmental Measures and International Trade and through its general procedures for bilateral and multilateral adjustment of differences;

— whenever possible (i.e. in cases which do not require immediate discontinuation of imports), countries should inform their trading partners in advance about the intended action in order that there might be an opportunity to consult within the G.A.T.T. Group on Environmental Measures and International Trade. Assistance in meeting consequences of stricter environmental standards ought to be given in the form of financial or technical assistance for research with the aim to remove the obstacles that the products of developing countries have encountered; — all countries agree that uniform environmental standards should not be expected to be applied universally by all countries with respect to given industrial processes or products except in those cases where environmental disruption may constitute a concern to other countries. Environmental standards should be established at whatever levels are necessary, to safeguard the environment and should not be aimed at gaining trade advantages.

Needless to say, principle 32 received enthusiastic support from the developing nations. It had been lifted directly from the crucial Founex report, which warned that "even if the developing countries were to regard the present environmental concern of the industrialized countries to be an irrelevant irritant, they can hardly remain indifferent to, or unaffected by it. Inevitably, the environmental concern will cast its shadow on all international economic relations." More specifically, the Founex report went on to make the gloomy prediction:

Many of the industrialized countries will be loath to see their production and employment suffer if their export prices rise as environmental standards are enforced; they may try to argue that imports from the developing countries based on less rigorous environmental standards should either be taxed or banned. The import-competing sectors and organized lobbies are likely to join in this outcry. Agricultural products may be the first to suffer. Some industrial products, notably chemicals, may fare no better. And from specifics, the argument can quickly go on to a general level. Why be liberal in admitting the products of the developing countries if they are the outgrowth of a "sweated environment"? The humanitarian concern for the environment can far too easily become a selfish argument for greater protectionism. The developing countries still confront the argument of "sweated labour": the argument of "sweated environment" will be equally fallacious but even harder to beat.

At the same time, however, most of the developing nations realized that there were several distinctions to be made. The raising of non-tariff barriers against their exports, particularly of foodstuffs, which might be designed to protect the health of consumers in the importing nation, could not legitimately be interpreted as a discriminatory move — above all where the standards used were accepted internationally. But serious disruptions could be avoided through prior consultation between the exporting and the importing nations concerning any new standards due to be imposed. In the same way, advance warning and consultation seemed to be the only protection against exports of developing countries such as lead and high-sulphur coal and oil which were likely to be increasingly displaced by the development of non-pollutive technology. Recycling was another development that might affect exports of the developing nations, but it could scarcely be considered as discrimination.

Despite these qualifications several industrialized nations, notably Canada, the U.S., and Britain, strongly opposed the idea of compensation for trade losses. Early in the debate, Canada, with the support of the other two, introduced an amendment to principle 32 with the following policy statement: "Canada recognizes that the adoption of environmental measures will have an impact on international trade flows. Canada does not agree that direct compensation should be given to protect the existing levels and patterns of trade. However, Canada is willing to provide assistance to developing countries to strengthen their economies and thus help offset the adverse impact on their development of measures adopted by the developing countries to protect their own environments." In supporting the amendment, the U.S. argued that "many forces affect export earnings and to single out any of these would be wrong in principle and a disincentive to environmental responsibility ..." Both arguments were based on a credo which has emerged in international negotiations concerning ocean dumping and pollution of the high seas, and holds that the polluter is responsible for paying for the damage he causes, a credo that is normally abbreviated in diplomatic shorthand to the "polluter pays" principle. Developing nations, however, argued loud and long that to expect the indigents of the world to accept financial responsibility in environmental trade upsets, on exactly the same basis as the wealthy industrial nations, was not only unfair but palpably absurd. The developing nations had their backs to the wall as it was.

The vehemence of their argument appeared to startle more than one delegation from the developed world, and led to Canada's reversing its position completely, much to the chagrin of its earlier allies. Canadian delegate Sen. Alan McNaughton explained at a press briefing that "our position had been that the polluter must pay. If we receive a shipment of food from a country and refuse entry to it because it doesn't meet our environmental standards, why should we have to pay compensation to the country that shipped it? . . . However, there was a distinct danger of a rift developing between the developing and developed nations over the issue which, so early in the convention, could have had disastrous results." Canada thus withdrew her first amendment, which would have removed all mention of compensation, and, through West Germany, sponsored a second one which left the thrust of the original document virtually untouched. Britain and the U.S., however, remained firm in their original opposition; the committee vote on the issue was 36 for, two (Britain and the U.S.) opposed and 11 abstentions. The developing nations had won a major victory, the significance of which could only increase in years to come. When the subject came before the plenary session on June 13 for final approval, Switzerland, Sweden, and Japan joined with the U.S. and Britain in abstaining from voting, but the clause still passed easily.

NOTES

1. *International Wildlife* magazine, April 1972.
2. The U.S. handles problems concerning international waterways shared between the U.S. and Canada through the International Joint Commission, established in 1908.

Swedish Anti-U.N. Demo

STOCKHOLM *(Staff) — Police clashed in Stockholm yesterday with about 300 anarchist demonstrators against the U.N. conference on the human environment.*

The demonstrators carried placards stating, "Unmask the United Nations Environmental Conference" and "Capitalism is the Cause of Environmental Ravages". A procession marched toward the old Parliament Buildings where the conference is being held. But about 200 policemen, including mounted officers, closed off all the streets leading to the building and dispersed the demonstrators with the help of dogs.

About 2,500 policemen are on duty during the conference. They fear organized demonstrations by various organizations which have stated their "distrust" of the U.N. The groups claim that the U.N. will not discuss the real problem of political and economic imbalance and the need for political change to solve environmental problems.

The Daily Telegraph (London), June 6, 1972

Chapter four

Under-development, over-development,
and the environment

Rhetoric to the contrary, it became clear very early in the Stockholm conference that several third-world nations were concerned less with issues, such as the alleged conflict between development and the environment, than with how those issues could be exploited to pry more foreign-aid money out of the rich. It was equally clear that their desperate plight made this attitude defensible.

To understand the position of these developing nations, it is useful to have some sort of mental picture of what "under-development" means for the 2-2½ billion for whom it is a way of life. Nearly ten years ago economist Robert Heilbroner tried to paint such a picture;[1] tragically, virtually nothing in his description, except population figures, has changed since then. Heilbroner outlined how a typical North American family, living in a small suburban home on an income of six or seven thousand dollars, could be transformed into an equally typical family of the under-developed world. First, the house is stripped of its furniture. Everything goes except the kitchen table, a few old blankets and a chair or two. The clothes filling the closets also go, save for each member of the family's oldest suit or dress and perhaps a couple of old shirts or blouses. Only one pair of shoes is left — for the head of the family. The rest will have to go without. In the kitchen all the appliances have, of course, already been removed. The cupboards are emptied, except for a box of matches, a bag of flour, some sugar, and salt. A few mouldy potatoes or other root vegetables are retrieved from the garbage to serve as the evening meal. To go with them there remain only a couple of onions and a handful of dried beans. The bathroom fixtures are dismantled and taken away (fewer than one quarter of Manila's low-income homes, for example, have toilets), the water turned off, the electricity disconnected. Next, the house itself goes. The family moves into the tool shed, or if they are lucky, perhaps the garage. In Hong Kong as in the metropolises of India, it is not uncommon for a family of four to live in an area no larger than that occupied by a single bed. In Seoul, Korea, a 1972 survey of housing showed that 36.9 per cent of low-income households occupy accommodation covering six to 12 square feet. Another 24 per cent of these families occupy 24 to 36 square feet, and the figures include kitchen and other utility spaces.

The average size of these households is 5½ persons. Still, our family is lucky to have any shelter at all. Well over a quarter of a million people in Calcutta live their lives out in the streets with no shelter whatever. Next, the rest of the houses in the suburb will have to go, to be replaced by shacks made by scrap materials of various kinds. Newspapers, magazines and books must also go, since virtually no one in the community can read them. (There are 100 million more adult illiterates now than 20 years ago.) Telephones must also be removed, but one radio for each 100 or so persons can stay. Government services like garbage collection, sewerage, mail delivery, fire protection, disappear also. Water comes from a pump at the end of the street and is likely to be contaminated by human and animal wastes. The nearest clinic is half a day's walk away and is run by a hastily-trained nurse or midwife. (In some developing countries, the doctor-patient ratio is worse than 1-50,000 as compared with 1-700 in the United States. Life expectancy is 40 per cent shorter than in the developed world. Child and infant mortality is four times as high.) To get to the clinic one takes a bicycle, if the family is fortunate enough to be able to afford one. If not, room can often be found on the roof of the local bus.

Whatever money the family had is naturally taken away, except, perhaps, for four or five dollars by way of provision for a rainy day. To bring in the family income of, say, 2-300 dollars a year, the father scrapes away at two or three acres of rocky, exhausted land. He is likely to be only a tenant farmer, which means that 30 per cent of his income goes to the landlord. Another ten per cent may go to pay off a debt with the local money lender. His efforts provide the family with perhaps 80 per cent of the minimum nourishment needed for full development — in a good year. If the children can get work, they may supplement the family income by a few cents a month doing piece-work, perhaps helping to make souvenirs for tourists. They can also beg or scavenge what they can, although they may not have to emulate those children in parts of Iran who have been found searching for undigested oats in the dung of horses. Once our typical North American family has been reduced to this level, it will have some idea of how most of the rest of the world lives. Its members will be fortunate that they are no worse off, because millions upon millions of the family of man are.

In their drive to develop, many poor nations have now added the environmental problems associated with industrial development and mechanized agriculture to the more traditional concerns of over-population and poverty. Afghanistan's national report, prepared for the Stockholm conference, expressed a new and growing concern for the proliferating use of long-lived pesticides, while pointing out at the same time that "two-thirds of our topsoil has been removed by erosion." This, the report says, "is due primarily to the widespread practice of one-crop planting and to the destruction of pastures by grazing of too many sheep and cattle per acre. Overgrazed areas of the country suffer from floods during the spring and dust storms during the summer and autumn." Kenya reported that "some districts have reached or exceeded their carrying capacity and our topsoil is disappearing far faster than it is created by natural weathering." At the same time, in some of the country's cities, particularly Nairobi, "the extent of air pollution from industrial vapours and particulate matter has reached the ... level where it is readily seen without the aid of instruments. There are other local climates within the vicinity of some factories where pollution is more dense — as in the case of the diatomite and cement plants — and their effect on the local ecology and human habitants is more readily noticeable. ... In Mombasa some two tons of sulphur (as SO_2) is emitted daily from the oil refinery ..." Swaziland noted a great reduction in bird life, which it attributed to the well-known effects of organochloride pesticides on bird reproduction. Iran reported: "It is possible that the face of the land has changed more significantly in the past two decades than it has in the entire balance of man's history in Iran. ... With its recent rapid industrial development Iran is no exception to the general pollution problem." In Turkey where, according to the national report, 45 per cent of the villages have either inadequate water supplies or no water supply at all, and where 70-75 per cent of the land is subject to erosion ranging from "severe" to "very severe", air pollution was also a "rather serious" problem in four urban centres. Describing a serious industrial water-pollution crisis, the Philippine report began: "Like leprosy in an advanced stage, the deterioration of [the Philippine] living environment can no longer be ignored ..."

The Burma report estimated that 90 per cent of the nation's households live in *basha*-type dwellings constructed mainly of bamboo and thatch, which

> usually last for about three years. They are attractive to ants and borer beetles, subjected to fire risks and receptive to fungus infestation. ... It has been conservatively estimated that about 65 per cent of the population in Rangoon live in slums or makeshift arrangements. The houses themselves are often little more than shacks or hovels, thrown together from cast-off materials. Smiths, bakers, tanners, cheroot rollers carry out their menial trade in and about their homes and most of the people prepare their food in open fires. Eyes are constantly smarting, throats irritated and lungs

affected. Although such conditions are not conducive to anyone's health, the risk seems to be greatest for the infants.

Incredibly, Burma reported well over 200,000 cases of leprosy, a preventable and curable disease. At the same time, the country's national report stated, "the spread of waste laden with lead and sulphur that spews from the Bowdin Mines at Namtu is spoiling vast areas of surrounding lands; the lead-filled industrial wastes that spurt from the battery factory at Kamayut are polluting land and water near by and the dust that gushes from the chimneys of the cement factory in Thayetmyo is devastating much arable land in the vicinity . . ." It was with all of this in mind that Maurice Strong had predicted: "The eco-catastrophes of which we hear so much are much more likely to occur in the developing world than in the wealthier countries that have the resources to deal with these problems."[2]

Several factors served to further complicate the already nightmarish predicament of the developing nations. In most countries, population and the work force tended to explode far ahead of industrialization. Joblessness was further increased by the importation of labour-saving technology by foreign-controlled firms in areas where cheap labour is the chief natural resource. Increased land consolidation brought on by modern agricultural technology, which operates efficiently only on large tracts of land, meant a steady flood of migrants into the cities, causing housing and other urban problems of staggering proportions. The social fabric, already stretched to the tearing point by these upheavals, was strained further by increased communication with the rich nations of the world, and the consequent "revolution of rising expectations". Moreover, the very dimensions of the problems facing these nations necessitated sweeping, disruptive reforms — there was no time for refinements. Nations that attempted to raise development capital through exports of raw materials were finding their markets shrivelled with increasing regularity by the development of synthetic substitutes in the rich nations. (In 1970, synthetic rubber production nearly equalled the world harvest of the natural product.) Other markets were blocked by giants of efficiency like Volkswagen, Mitsui, and I. T. & T.

Despite all of this, the rhetoric of optimism was, predictably, much in evidence at Stockholm, particularly among the developed nations and their representatives on international institutions. For what was there to be gained by being pessimistic? Robert S. McNamara, formerly U.S. defence secretary and now President of the World Bank group, expressed the conventional wisdom of the technocrats in his speech to the convention plenary:

While the issues before us are serious, they are not beyond solution. Intensified research, precise analysis, and day-to-day action are what they most require. What they least require are anxious speculation and alarmist accusation. . . . [The] dilemma is this: the achievement of a level of life in accord with fundamental human dignity for the world's two and three-quarter billion poor is simply not possible without the continued economic growth of the developing nations, and the developed nations as well. But economic growth on the pattern of the past — and most particularly that in the already highly-industrialized wealthy nations — poses an undeniable threat to the environment and to the health of man.

Happily, McNamara affirmed, "there is no evidence that the economic growth which the developing countries so desperately require will necessarily involve an unacceptable burden on either their own or anybody else's environment." He went on to explain how the World Bank had recently established the post of environmental advisor

with a strong mandate to review and evaluate every investment project from the standpoint of its effects on the environment. . . . By careful analysis we have found, in every instance to date, that we can reduce the danger of environmental hazards either at no cost to the project or at a cost so moderate that the borrower has been fully agreeable to accepting the necessary safeguards. Central to the success of this approach is the principle that in the issue of environmental damage, prevention is infinitely to be preferred to cure. Not only is it more effective, but it is clearly less expensive. . . . Our experience is that environmental protection can be built into development projects as competently and successfully as any other requisite element. . . . Each project processed in the bank is now reviewed by the Environment Office, and a careful in-house study is made of the ecological components. If the project warrants it, an on-site "ecological reconnaissance" study is commissioned by the Bank with the use of qualified consultants. If more serious problems are uncovered, a still more intensive on-site evaluation is undertaken in order to determine what specialized solutions should be incorporated into the project's specifications. While in principle the Bank could refuse a loan on environmental grounds — in a situation, for example, in which the problems are of such severity that adequate safeguards cannot be applied, or in which the borrower is wholly unwilling to take reasonable measures in his own interest — the fact is that no such case has yet arisen. Since initiating our environmental review, we have found that in every instance the recommended safeguards can and have been successfully negotiated and implemented.

McNamara's viewpoint was a valuable one, if only for its representative nature. But it was also undeniably narrow, and generated much crit-

icism, particularly among trained environmentalists. A brochure prepared by the World Bank for distribution in Stockholm ("The World
Bank and the World Environment") contained several case studies.
One, concerning Dubrovnik in Yugoslavia, was particularly revealing.
Alluding to the fact that fish stocks in the Adriatic have been seriously
depleted in recent times by large-scale dumping of municipal and industrial wastes, the study reports the World Bank's role in a related
project. It is worth quoting at some length because it helps illuminate
the bank's somewhat confined perspective:

> The fish aren't running like they used to in the Adriatic Sea. As
> long as five years ago, the Food and Agriculture Organization
> (F.A.O.) sounded the warning that the Adriatic was in trouble.
> Things haven't improved much since then in that beautiful body
> of water separating Italy from Yugoslavia.
>
> The waters of the south Adriatic are particularly and intensely
> blue near the Yugoslavian city of Dubrovnik. They are also pol-
> luted.
>
> Dubrovnik — the old, walled portion of the city of 30,000 people
> has been carefully preserved since its reconstruction after the great
> earthquake of 1667 — has an old sewerage system. In fact, it's about
> 2,000 years old, built by sanitary engineers from the Roman
> Empire.
>
> The system was recently extended for a distance of about four
> kilometres, so that raw sewage would empty into the Adriatic Sea
> by the tip of a peninsula lying to the north of the old city.
>
> And it is on that tip that Yugoslavia, with the help of World
> Bank financing, is to build one of the largest tourism complexes
> in the world, a complex which includes nine hotels with beds for
> 5,000 people, sport and recreation facilities, restaurants, shops and
> night clubs.
>
> Tourist revenues are of great importance to Yugoslavia's eco-
> nomic development. More than 3.5 per cent of the country's total
> work force can trace its employment directly to the tourism in-
> dustry. A total of 30 million visitors to Yugoslavia in 1969 left
> behind more than $300 million in foreign exchange.
>
> Yugoslavia hopes to triple that figure by 1975. And the planned
> "Babin Kuk" resort near Dubrovnik figures importantly in those
> hopes.
>
> But a $20-million investment in a massive recreational facility
> which, at the same time, might be subject to hazardous pollutants
> is not an investment at all, but a gamble. No studies had ever been
> made to determine what the effect of additional raw sewage on the
> marine biota in the Dubrovnik area might be. No studies on the
> tidal movements and currents in the tourist complex area had been
> made, and therefore, no guarantee could be made that sewage
> would not befoul the beaches and waters of the peninsula.

The World Bank, its consultants, and the Yugoslav marine biology station at Dubrovnik, got together to come up with a plan to minimize the effects on the marine environment by the development of Babin Kuk.

The plans have been drawn up. Sewer outlets have been designed to keep wastes out of the area, leaving the waters clean for swimming and boating. The Yugoslav government is also planning to modernize — at a cost of $8 million — the sewerage system for the entire city of Dubrovnik.

People come to Dubrovnik because, for centuries, it has not changed. But change accompanies people as inevitably as their baggage. The Bank and the Yugoslav government are determined that changing Dubrovnik without changing Dubrovnik is one petard upon which they must not be hoisted.

The glib obfuscation of this breathless piece of Madison Avenue-ese could not hide the following facts: the Adriatic is already seriously polluted; the bank's plans for extending outlets for raw sewage farther out into the Adriatic will in no way improve this condition — only an expensive sewage-treatment plant could do that. This the bank was apparently not willing to press for. The plans serve only to protect in the narrowest aesthetic sense, and in the short term, the immediate investment at Babin Kuk. The other case histories described in the pamphlet could be analyzed with similar results.

McNamara's position received reinforcement from a resource paper drafted for the conference by the U.N. Industrial Development Organization (U.N.I.D.O.). "Industrialization," the report stated,

is often one of the major solutions to the problems of poverty and underdevelopment. Industrial development can indeed become a major solution to these problems with the incorporation of environmental criteria and goals. In this context, there need not be a major conflict between development and maintaining a desirable human environment. Each country will have to decide, in the light of its own situation and development strategy, the policy it wishes to follow. Industrialization generally results in the release of pollutants and wastes, and thus reacts on the environment in many ways. However, with appropriate planning, management and control, the detrimental impact upon the environment can be minimized.

The report went on to list a number of techniques that could be used by developing nations. Proper physical and economic planning would mean that climatic and topographical considerations would be taken into account when planning new industrial sites, "so that the effects of pollutants, odours and noise on human settlements may be minimized or altogether eliminated. For example, an industrial plant may be located so that the prevailing winds may disperse potential pollutants away from neighbouring cities." Deliberate decentralization of industrial development — establishing industrial estates well away from the large cities — would not only help disperse pollution, but also relieve the pressure of migration from rural areas being experienced by cities in all developing countries. The report also pointed out that particular production techniques used by an industry can often be tailored to the local social and physical environment:

> In many cases intermediate technologies, with high labour demands, small plant size and less reliance on energy are often more appropriate to the needs of developing countries than sophisticated, capital-intensive processes requiring highly-trained workers. . . . On the other hand, the sophisticated capital-intensive technologies may produce less pollution because of increased efficiency and automation. For example, large-scale highly-mechanized canning operations may be preferable to small-scale labour-intensive canning operations.

Re-use and recycling techniques could be designed into new industrial plants for only a small portion of the overall capital cost. The deliberate decision could be taken to produce end products which have a long life, as opposed to those aimed at early obsolescence. Both measures would reduce pollution and lower demand for scarce or expensive raw materials.

Other expedients could offer developing nations the hope not only of being able to avoid the environmental mistakes of the rich nations but also, at long last, of gaining a more equitable share of the world's wealth. One of the more significant, if controversial palliatives was suggested in the conference working paper on development and the environment. The relevant paragraph was titled "International distribution of industry":

> The need of developing countries to establish certain basic industries (petroleum and chemicals, metal extracting and processing, pulp and paper and others) coincides with a growing concern of industrialized countries for the environmental degradation which arises from heavy concentration of such industries in their countries. These provide a new reason for re-examining the factors which determine the location of industries internationally, and, in turn, open up new opportunities and new risks for developing countries. The capacity of the natural environment to absorb and dissipate waste without suffering intolerable damage must now be regarded as an economic [rather than a "free"] resource. Since the

less industrialized countries have by and large put lighter burdens on their environment resources than the industrialized countries and may therefore be able to afford less stringent environmental standards, this could give them a comparative advantage in the establishment of certain new industries. Such new activities could have a significant impact on development through increasing income, productivity and employment which would subsequently increase the ability of the countries concerned to improve the environment. However, countries in considering such opportunities should also take full account of the potential risk of environmental damage which might affect development gains. In many cases it should be possible to avoid or mitigate such risks by adequate planning, locations and use of proper technologies. In order to avoid the indiscriminate import of pollution, developing countries could enforce environmental standards to achieve minimal levels of industrial pollution in the light of their stages of development and of their cultural and social objectives.

The paper went on to recommend that governments of developing countries "consider fully" this argument, and that the secretary-general of the U.N. assist these nations in taking advantage of opportunities that might appear.

Considering the almost revolutionary nature of this argument — that industry might be distributed throughout the world in a coherent manner which would take more account of its impact on the local environment than of its ownership — many observers at Stockholm were surprised when it passed the final plenary stage easily, by a vote of 65-0-8 (with the U.S. prominent among the eight abstainers). The developing nations could now have at least some hope that their relatively unstressed atmospheres and hydrospheres might provide them with the competitive advantage needed to begin to compete more equally for their fair share of gross world production. Nor were they unaware, on the whole, of the risks inherent in such a policy. During committee discussions the Ghanaian delegation, among others, warned that the poor nations of the world "would not take too much of what is not wanted elsewhere," and that the rich nations would not be allowed to "dump" polluting industries abroad. The delegation leader argued that developed nations had a responsibility to see that branch plants established overseas behaved in an environmentally responsible manner. Note was also taken of the fact that such a policy would make it all the more urgent for the developing nations to quickly establish comprehensive environmental standards. Once again the example of Brazil was there to demonstrate the damage that could be done in the absence of such guidelines. The consensus was that industrial transfer from rich to poor

nations would be acceptable, if the foreign investment was on favourable terms and conditions, if it added to the net transfer of resources
from rich to poor nations, if it conformed to the environmental standards of the recipient country. So long as these safeguards were provided,
in the words of the Founex report, "there is no reason why the developing countries should not increasingly specialize in certain industrial
fields, both for home market production and export purposes, which
are going to become more costly for the industrialized world because
of their growing concern with environmental standards."

Because of the remarkable thoroughness of the work of the preparatory committee, delegates to the Stockholm conference seldom
found it necessary to propose major additions to the recommendations
contained in the working papers prepared for their discussion. However, in the area of development and the environment, one such addition was made, and subsequently approved in plenary. It suggested that
"the secretary-general, in co-operation with other international bodies
as appropriate, should examine the extent to which the problems of
pollution could be ameliorated by a reduction in the current levels of
production and in the future rate of growth of the production of synthetic products and substitutes which, in their natural form, could be
produced by developing countries; and make recommendations for
national and international action. . . ."

The reasoning behind this proposal was well illustrated in an article
published just prior to the conference by U.S. biologist and environmentalist Barry Commoner.[3] Commoner chose rubber as an example of
a natural product that had been widely displaced by synthetic substitutes. Before World War II, all of the world's rubber came from the
latex of the rubber tree, which flourished naturally and on plantations
in its native ecosystem of the tropics. The energy required to produce
rubber in this way, he pointed out, came from a constantly renewable
source — the sun — and the product was generated in a non-pollutive
way within the plant itself. As an added bonus, the tree produced
oxygen. Manufacturing synthetic rubber, on the other hand, required
vast amounts of energy usually derived from non-renewable resources —
fossil fuels — whose combustion polluted the atmosphere. The synthetic
rubber itself was made from a non-renewable and increasingly scarce
resource — petroleum. Moreover, the production of natural rubber employed large numbers of relatively unskilled workers, and so helped to
solve the terrible unemployment problems of the poor, tropical nations,
while synthetic production was more capital-intensive, and centred in
the developed world. Why, then, was it that in 1970, U.S. production of

synthetic rubber had come to nearly equal world production of natural rubber? The answer, as is the case with many of our most destructive and irrational decisions, lay in the exigencies of war. Neither the Axis powers nor the Allies of World War II produced any natural rubber. The obvious military drawbacks of this situation led both Germany and the U.S. to develop and begin producing the synthetic substitute. After the war, arguments of national security succeeded in keeping the synthetic factories open. The Korean War gave added impetus to their efforts, as did the cold war. Huge stockpiles of both synthetic and natural rubber were hoarded in the U.S. As tension cooled around 1960, these American stockpiles were sold off, with predictable results — between 1960 and 1970, the price of natural rubber fell from 43 to 23 cents a pound. In Malaysia, a 30 per cent increase in rubber production between 1960 and 1968 could not prevent the total market value of the crop from dropping by 33 per cent. Ecological sanity, Commoner observed, would demand a return to natural rubber. The usual argument against this — that natural rubber production could not meet world demand — he dismissed as specious. To meet total world demand, natural rubber output would have to be trebled. Increased efficiency, along with wider use of new, more productive, genetic strains, would make this goal wholly attainable. In the event, however, the U.S. decision to abstain from voting on this recommendation made it clear that strategic military considerations were still powerful determinants of national policy.

Perhaps the best hope held out to developing nations by the Stockholm conference was that the new concern for the protection and enhancement of the human environment might lead to a renewed international effort to eliminate human degradation and poverty. As the Founex report put it: "An emerging understanding of the indivisibility of the earth's natural systems on the part of the rich nations could help strengthen the vision of a human family, and even encourage an increase in aid to poor nations' efforts to improve and protect their part of the global household." A more blunt statement of the same idea might point out that where altruism had demonstrably failed to pry anything resembling an adequate foreign-aid budget out of the world's rich nations, perhaps fear for their own survival would. Once it was realized that people are part of their own environment, and that an environmental disaster anywhere in the global system would have repercussions throughout the system, rich nations might finally, if only to protect their own interests, see fit to do something significant about improving the human environment in the third world.

Given that a true comprehension of environmental issues must include an understanding of the concept of limits to growth, such an understanding carries with it a renewed injunction to serve justice in dividing the planet's wealth more equitably among its inhabitants. Only so long as it was assumed that the Earth's resources were infinite could the question, "Where must the restraints be placed," be avoided. Only then could it be assumed, as McNamara assumed, that the ever-increasing wealth of the industrialized world would trickle down in amounts ever increasing to the poor nations, until at last they achieved something like a reasonable standard of living. But there were limits, and what is more, they were being approached too rapidly to allow for our time-honoured complacency. Restraints were demonstrably needed. Were they to be placed on the necessities of the poor, or on the luxuries of the rich? The issues could no more be avoided than the scientific imperative from which they sprang — the concept of limits to growth. In the words of Barbara Ward:

> We can cheat on morals. We can cheat on politics. We can deceive ourselves with dreams and myths. But there is no mon-keying about with DNA or photosynthesis or eutrophication or nuclear fusion or the impact on all living things of excessive radia-tion — from the sun or the hydrogen bomb. And what our in-credible scientific breakthroughs of the last century have taught us is that the ultimate energy of the universe both sustains or destroys life and that the mechanisms and balances by which it becomes life-enhancing are fragile and precious beyond our belief. To act without rapacity, to use knowledge with wisdom, to respect inter-dependence, to operate without hubris and greed are not simply moral imperatives. They are an accurate scientific description of the means of survival.[4]

Unfortunately, the notion of limits to growth was nowhere to be found in conference documentation directly concerning the voting delegates. So there was no way of gauging how, or even whether, it had influenced their thinking, either with regard to the broad question of international redistribution of wealth or the narrower question of the likely long-term prospects of any individual nation committed to perpetual growth.

L. Sico Mansholt, president of the European Economic Community, was one of the very few at Stockholm to come to grips with the ques-tion of justifying industrial growth beyond certain limits in the already highly-developed nations. Mansholt was already well known for his views on the dangers of unrestrained economic growth in the developed world. Just weeks before the conference he had stirred up considerable controversy in the Common Market by arguing that the world could not survive if Europe and America continued to increase their material wealth at their present rate, and suggesting that the ideal of economic growth reflected in the notion of gross national product (G.N.P.) be replaced by other priorities, which he lumped under the label of "gross national happiness". In his speech to the conference plenary session, Mansholt asked:

> Can we in the West, taking account of the finite nature of our world in which natural resources and energy are limited by the very nature of the world's ecosystem, can we continue to pursue economic growth on the present pattern? The reply to this question could very well be crucial if we are to make the world habitable. Many people, to avoid certain unpleasant conclusions, use the following reasoning: we must adopt means of production which do not pollute and which avoid the waste of natural resources. To do this we need to make large investments in expensive (non-polluting) technology and this means further growth is needed — this extra growth must be used to implement certain private and public, national and international measures necessary to create an inhabitable world.
>
> But one can ask if all this is possible any more, given on the one hand the depletion of resources, on the other the resulting need to cause 75 per cent of the world's population to exist at a much lower standard of living than our own, and given above all the obligation to permit the developing nations to develop their own non-polluting industries. The organs of the U.N. are going to have to specify exactly what standard of living this 75 per cent of the world population can actually reach, taking into account the limits of resources and energy and the equilibrium of the ecosphere. And if we are to be sincere in our promise to close the gap between the rich and poor nations we must be ready to accept the consequences for our own rate of growth and its direction.
>
> Thus it is time to ask: Are our present social structures and production methods defensible? And what about the problem of the struggle to safeguard the environment? Are we ready — we in the rich countries — to face the consequences? Or will we rather hide behind the struggle to cure the symptoms in order to avoid answering the question? I hope the U.N. will not hesitate to try to shed light on this problem.
>
> And what, in practice, happens as a result of the statement: first economic growth and then we will be able to finance extra public investment to improve the quality of life? We have had experience in this matter in the European Economic Community. During the period 1965-70 we had as an objective for public investments a growth rate double that of the community's G.N.P. That is, a growth of G.N.P. of four per cent was to be followed by an increase in public investment of eight per cent. Despite the fact that the growth of G.N.P. was actually five per cent per year, that is to

say, greater than the four per cent forecast, investment in the public sector did not increase; it remained at a level of five per cent. In fact, public investment was sacrificed to the fight against inflation. Five years of experience has shown us just how difficult it is to accomplish a large programme of public investment for the protection of the environment.

The "consequences" referred to by Mansholt are by now familiar: if the limits to the economic growth of the rich nations were within sight, then rich nations would no longer be able to argue that by continuing to grow they generate the wealth needed to help the developing nations raise the economic standards of their inhabitants. A real net transfer of wealth between the rich and poor nations would thus be necessary: that is to say, the rich nations would have to become a little poorer to make the poor nations richer. The same consequences applied within each nation as well. Governments that had for centuries placated their poor by raising the total national income without closing the gap between rich and poor citizens would be forced, finally, to face the question of income disparities. Growth would no longer be able to be used as a substitute for equality. In a state, as in a world, that had reached the limits to its economic growth, there had to be a ceiling on affluence. And presumably men would also wish to establish a floor below which no one would be allowed to fall. It followed that, the higher the lower limit below which no one is allowed to fall, the lower must be the upper limit above which no one can rise. It had been argued that the western nations' fear of such a situation was the main cause of their addiction to growth at virtually any cost. It seemed clear, in any case, that a more equal distribution of wealth would go a long way towards curing the mania for growth, since one's apprehension of how "poor" or "disadvantaged" one is in a rich country depended almost entirely on how well the Joneses were doing.

If the U.S. and, to a lesser extent, the rest of the western industrialized nations had fallen headlong into the "first growth, then public investment" syndrome described by Mansholt, there was more than one highly developed nation that had begun to see the suicidal aspects of such a policy. Britain's Secretary of State for the Environment, Peter Walker, was among those who gave tentative acknowledgment to the need to break the growth cycle. "We stand today where men stood at the Renaissance," Mr. Walker told the conference:

> We, like them, cannot depend on traditional ways of doing things. We need to face the logic of scientific understanding. If research teaches us that a trend we now see could lead to devastation in thirty years, the fact that it can only be averted by an unpre-

cedented response is irrelevant. We need the adventurousness — the daring — of a new Renaissance in our political thinking. This is one reason why my government has decided on a study by my department of long-term trends in the factors affecting the human situation, and ways of predicting them. We are not persuaded by everything that has been said about these matters lately — or by the models so far developed — but we do feel that these are such important issues we must give them proper attention.

Unfortunately, Walker was to destroy much of his credibility by insisting at a later press conference that his government's decision to go ahead with Concorde, in the face of firm evidence of its potential danger to the environment, was in no way inconsistent with the sentiments expressed above.

It was left to Japan, that prodigy of economic growth so much admired in the West, to paint an uncompromisingly frank picture of a people who had placed growth above all else — to give the assembled nations the same kind of perspective on development that Heilbroner had provided on under-development. Background papers and case studies prepared for the conference presented a sobering catalogue of human suffering. Mercury poisoning had affected as many as 15,000 Japanese, killing hundreds and leaving others afflicted with severe neurological disturbances and loss of motor control similar to that experienced in cerebral apoplexy or encephalitis, severe disturbance of speech, narrowness of the field of vision, deafness, and other sensory disturbances. A number of children had been born horribly deformed or retarded after their mothers had been poisoned by the metal. Their affliction was known as "Minimata disease", after the bay just south of Nagasaki which had supplied the tainted seafood that caused it, contaminated by industrial wastes dumped untreated into the sea. Nearly three hundred other Japanese had been affected by "Itai-Itai" ("Ouch-Ouch") disease — cadmium poisoning. It was so named because the slightest movement by the affected person causes him excruciating pain. Calcium in the body is removed by the disease, leaving bones as thin and delicate as eggshells. Breaks occur frequently: X-ray photographs of one patient revealed 72 fractures. Ten thousand more Japanese have been poisoned by PCBS (polycholorobiphenyls), a chemical group used widely in industrial processes. As a result they have suffered to varying extents from such symptoms as changes in pigmentation, acne-form eruptions, loss of hair, general fatigue, poor eyesight, vomiting, asthma-like respiratory distress, headache, stomach ache, loss of memory, and reduced ability to concentrate. Tens of thousands of Japanese suffer from serious respiratory diseases, caused by air pollution, which periodically force school closings and make it mandatory for traffic policemen in some areas to wear gas masks on duty. Photochemical smog from automobile exhaust (so-called "Los Angeles smog") has become the subject of frequent public warnings in Tokyo's news media. People are asked not to use their cars or operate other facilities which might add to the problem, while sound cars patrol heavily-affected areas to warn children to avoid excessive exercise. Entire classrooms of students have been hospitalized after continuing to play because they missed the warnings, and national newspapers have compared the situation to the air-raid alerts of the Second World War. Just as the economic growth rates of all other developed nations paled in comparison with those of the Japanese, so did their problems with environmental pollution of all kinds.

The Japanese delegates to the Stockholm conference were a chastened group. "We who had firmly believed since the war that greater production and higher G.N.P. were the ways to happiness," that country's environment minister told the conference plenary, "have been sorely disillusioned." The despoiling of nature by industry has led, he said, to a degradation of the spirit. In a country whose art had for centuries delighted in what was most delicate and fragile, the people were now "not even aware that they are losing their feeling for nature". The Japanese had begun seriously to ask the question: G.N.P. for whom, for what? "We must reorient our priorities from a worship of G.N.P. to a respect for human life," the environment minister said.

Those familiar with the Japanese experience knew this to be more than just the usual empty rhetoric, for the country's government had for some months been seriously studying ways to replace G.N.P. with a measure of Net National Welfare (N.N.W.). The decision not to introduce this study at the Stockholm conference was unfortunate and inexplicable. It could have helped to fill one of the larger gaps in the conference's deliberations. It was in the developed nations that revisions to the G.N.P. concept were most urgently demanded, yet whenever this need was recognized in conference recommendations it was with specific reference to the developing nations. The Japanese chose following the conference to report their studies to the Organization for Economic Co-operation and Development (O.E.C.D.). The awkwardly-translated preliminary report outlined several aspects of the problem:

> *Reclassification of G.N.P. according to social goals:* The present G.N.P. is constituted in such a way that it represents "who" (government, enterprise, households, etc.) bought how much of "what" (consumer goods, capital goods, etc.). Adding "for what", the social

targets (people's needs) to them, the G.N.P. is going to be reclass-
ified, so that it would give us a clue for finding new targets in
economic planning ... not only to see for what social goals (for
instance, health, education, etc.) the present G.N.P. is spent, but
also ... to see for what social targets the resources available in the
future G.N.P. should be allocated.

Strengthening G.N.P. as a welfare index: The [function of]
G.N.P. concepts ... looked at from the point of view of people's
welfare ... is not sufficient. The reason why ... cannot be ascribed
to the problem of the so-called "disproduct" and to factors of welfare which are not reflected in G.N.P. [Expenditures] for prevention of pollution, recovery from damage [caused] by pollution, pro-
longation of commuting distances due to urbanization, traffic accidents, etc., are included as components of G.N.P. They are not
necessarily making a net contribution to improvement of welfare.
Pollution of [the] natural environment (air, water, natural views,
etc.) ... [is] either not taken into consideration by the present
system of national accounts at all, or some part of it has even been
included as [a] positive factor in the calculation of G.N.P. ... From
the point of view of welfare, such pollutions and depletion of assets
should be deducted. ... Such negative factors in the present calculation of G.N.P. as shortening of working hours (increase of free
time) can be positive factors for the improvement of welfare.

Change from flow economics to stock economics: This is an
approach from social stocks, [on] which people's welfare depends
heavily ... the social stock used here does not only mean "the
stock of goods" in the narrow sense, as opposed to the "flow" concept in the traditional economics, but contains also ... stocks which
relate to more sophisticated wants of man. ... They were divided
into six items: natural stock (e.g. air and water pollution, decrease
of natural views); social overhead capital stock (e.g. consumers'
durable goods, clothes, personal effects); personnel stock (e.g.
teachers, medical doctors); cultural stock (e.g. cultural goods, communications media); social institutional stock (e.g. social security
systems).

Non-monetary approach to a welfare index: Among the items
which [make up] people's living and welfare, some items are difficult to express in monetary terms ... for instance nutrition,
health, education, leisure, safety ... which may be expressed quantitatively in some form or other.[5]

To the extent that the Stockholm conference avoided such areas of
controversy, one could comment with some justice that in its largely
successful attempt to make itself relevant to the developing nations it
had decreased its direct relevance for the developed world. Perhaps that
was as it should be. There was no shortage of readily accessible information on the special problems of the developed nations. What was

important was to point out to the rest of the world ways to avoid making the same mistakes. Thus, to say that the conference documents did
not take adequate notice of the special growth-related problems of the
developed nations is not to say that the conference documents failed to
question the advisability of wholesale adoption of western-style industrialization by the developing third world. This is borne out by a paragraph that occurs in the "Statement of Issues" section of the conference
working paper on development and the environment:

> While development is a necessary precondition for overcoming
> many of the environmental problems of poor societies, this is not
> to say that such problems could be automatically and spontaneously
> resolved by the mere acceleration of economic growth. There is, on
> the contrary, ample evidence to suggest that certain patterns of
> economic growth could bring in their wake not the solution but
> the aggravation of acute social and environmental problems. His-
> torically, economic growth has in many cases been accompanied by
> rising unemployment, greater inequality and increasing poverty
> and ill health for large sections of the populations of the devel-
> oping countries. There is increasing awareness of the limitations
> evident in the narrowly-focused pursuit of the goal of raising
> G.N.P.

Plenary-session statements by many, if not most, representatives of
developing nations echoed this point of view. Nowhere, however, did
either the conference papers or any of the national delegates go so far as
to state the facts baldly — to point out that it was very probably not
possible for the planet to support even its present population if everyone were allowed to attain the level of consumption enjoyed by the
inhabitants of the rich nations. For that would have raised the un-
askable question: "How much longer will the industrial nations be able
to afford their own profligacy, and how much longer will the other
nations of the world permit them to do so?"

It is possible to argue that many of the major flaws in the conference's dealings with the question of development and the environment, particularly as it related to the developing nations, stemmed
from the fact that "development" was never clearly redefined in the
light of the new awareness of man's relation with his environment. The
inadequacy of earlier definitions is apparent in this widely-accepted
interpretation, propounded by David Blelloch in 1958[6]: "The distin-
guishing feature of a developed society is that it has evolved a social
and administrative organization, a system of education, a relationship
between classes and sexes, a set of habits and customs, a way of life and
a scale of values which are compatible with modern industrial tech-

nology and the mass production and distribution of commodities which it implies." In other words, "development" means "industrialization". In so far as it can be assumed that Blelloch, and others who defined the word in similar terms, would agree that the aim of development is to improve the quality of existence of the inhabitants of the developing nations, it is clear that they have made the assumption that industrialization is the only route to a better quality of life. It is reasonable to ask, however, if "modern" industrialization is indeed the only way, or if it is even the best way. According to at least one commentator,[7] such a belief is based on a number of misapprehensions. It assumes, first of all, that industrialization in Europe and North America took place in an ordered manner designed to achieve a goal set by the people. It should thus be possible for people in developing nations to set goals and achieve them by copying the pattern of industrial growth of the rich nations. The fact is, however, that industrialization in the rich nations was "the result of a series of historical accidents, responses to particular and immediate stimuli and the application of existing scientific knowledge to the solving of immediate problems. It was a hand-to-mouth process based on no discernible plan."[8] A case in point might be the decision of the developed nations to opt for nuclear power as a replacement for increasingly scarce supplies of hydro-electric and fossil fuel energy resources. As anyone might suspect who is aware of the very serious problems of long-term storage of highly toxic radioactive wastes, this decision was not taken in terms of what was best for human welfare after any exhaustive examination of alternatives. It was taken because atomic reactors were needed to produce nuclear weapons. Nuclear power stations became a relatively inexpensive "spin-off" worth taking advantage of. It now seems quite probable that if this had not been the case, the potential dangers of fission reactors to human health might have caused us to wait for the non-polluting fusion reactor before going into the nuclear-power business. Solar, tidal, or even geo-thermal power would have been much more likely candidates to fill the gap.

Further, the belief assumes that the process of industrialization was successful in achieving the goal of a high quality of existence for the inhabitants of the industrialized nation, and that it will continue to be so. But as pointed out by "development and the environment" paper quoted above, poverty, unemployment and poor health remain problems for large segments of even the most industrially advanced states, and these problems do not seem to be amenable to solution by further industrialization on the accepted pattern. Moreover, "it should be remembered that beyond a level of bare subsistence poverty is a condition

China Puts a Spanner in the Works

STOCKHOLM — *China erupted this morning with devastating force at the U.N. environment conference here with a blistering attack on the Vietnam war and the way that "policies of plunder, aggression and war frenziedly pursued by the super-powers" had become the main cause "of increasingly serious pollution and damage to the human environment".*

In China's first major intervention at the conference — a 45-minute speech to the special plenary session — the leader of the Chinese delegation, Tank-ke, outlined the main points of principle that China is now insisting should be included in the official declaration on the human environment. These points amount to such a radical attack on the developed countries, and raise such fundamental economic and social issues, it is now most unlikely that a conference declaration will ever be agreed . . .

Observers here are frankly astounded by the vehemence of China's outburst. The greatest fear is that it will wreck any hopes of reaching an agreed declaration, which has already had some 20 amendments submitted to it since Thursday morning when China forced and then won a unanimous vote that the declaration should be re-drafted by an all-nation working group.

The Observer (London), June 11, 1972

Chapter five

*Environmental ethics:
the Draft Declaration*

The draft Declaration on the Human Environment, the shortest of the conference working papers, proved to be an authentic "sleeper". Planned originally as a relatively innocuous generalized statement of those principles which were so widely accepted as to provoke little serious argument — a sort of lowest ethical common denominator — it spawned so much controversy that the conference nearly foundered over the attempt to have it accepted.

The idea of a declaration was first put forward during an initial meeting of the preparatory committee in New York during March, 1970. It was to be "a document of basic principles", which would "stimulate public opinion and community participation for the protection and betterment of the human environment", and "provide guiding principles for governments in their formulation of policy and set objectives for future international co-operation". Members of the preparatory committee were left to mull over their ideas for a declaration of this type until the next meeting, held in Geneva during February, 1971. At that time the conference was still being considered within the original, 1968, terms of reference — that is, its primary purpose was still seen to be education and dissemination of knowledge. It was not until the committee met for the third time in September of 1971 that it had become clear that the job of educating the public and their political leaders had already been partly accomplished through the explosion of public interest in environmental matters, and that the Stockholm conference would have to produce some concrete action if it were to be taken seriously by observers around the world. So while it was widely recognized at that second preparatory committee meeting that the declaration might prove to be one of the more important conference documents, its projected significance was seen more in terms of its potential value as an educational and inspirational tool than in terms of any legal weight it might carry. In fact, the committee was quite explicit in its feeling that the document should not "formulate legally binding provisions". In any case, the intergovernmental working group (I.W.G.) set up at that meeting to draft the declaration was left open-ended: membership was to include all 27 members of the preparatory committee, but any other U.N. member nation that wished to be involved in the drafting process was invited to take part. It was hoped that by making membership on the I.W.G. as broadly representative as possible the final document might be spared the effects of destructive wrangling at Stockholm and could thus be presented to the public in pristine purity, a lofty environmental ethic that could soar above politics.

The I.W.G. worked steadily for nearly a year from the time of its first meeting in March, 1971, to put the declaration together. Discussion centred around drafts presented by several nations and eventually hammered into a single document on which broad consensus could be achieved. Canada, the U.S., and Sweden were among the first nations to present proposals to the working group. While the documents produced by Sweden and the U.S. were innocuous in the extreme (described as "shocking non-declarations" by one participant), the Canadian paper made it clear Canada supported the position, taken by several of the developing nations, that the declaration should be a strong statement containing a solid foundation for the future development of international environmental law. The U.S. was eventually won over to a lukewarm acceptance of the position adopted by Canada. Sweden remained intransigent. After a brief preamble, the Canadian draft went on to state nine principles:

> 1) Every state has a sovereign and inalienable right to its environment, including its land, air and water and to dispose of its natural resources.
> 2) Every state has a right to environmental integrity corresponding to its right to territorial integrity.
> 3) Every state has the right to take all necessary and appropriate measures to protect its environmental integrity.
> 4) Every state has a duty to conduct its activities with due regard to their effects upon the environment of other states.
> 5) No state may use or permit the use of its territory in such a manner as to cause damage to the environment of other states or to the environment of areas beyond the limits of national jurisdiction.
> 6) No state may use areas beyond the limits of national jurisdiction in such a manner as to cause damage to the environment of such areas or to the environment of other states.
> 7) Every state has the responsibility to compensate for damage caused by such activities.
> 8) Every state has a duty to consult with other states before undertaking activities which may damage the environment of such states, and a similar duty to consult with the appropriate international organization, if any, before undertaking activities which may damage the environment in areas beyond the limits of national jurisdiction.

9) Every state has a duty to ensure that national activities are carried out in conformity with the principles set forth in this declaration.

While the first three principles closely resembled the existing provisions of the charter of the U.N. and were thus already generally accepted tenets of international law, principles 4–8 contained three important new legal precepts: states must not pollute the environment of their neighbours or the shared environment beyond national boundaries (i.e. the seas and the atmosphere); before embarking on undertakings which might damage the environment of neighbouring jurisdictions, states must consult with the neighbours concerned; states who cause damage to the environment of others must compensate the affected states for the damage. It was to the credit of the I.W.G. that the draft declaration which finally emerged from their deliberations contained all three legal principles in almost undiluted form (Appendix 2). Despite its ambiguities, irrelevancies, and inelegant prose, it had punch. The uneasy nature of the consensus achieved within the I.W.G. was reflected in the fact that the group handed the document over to the fourth meeting of the preparatory committee in March, 1972, as if it were a piece of Dresden china, and the committee passed it on to the Stockholm secretariat gingerly, with the proviso that "the agreement to forward the text to the conference did not imply any expression of approval or disapproval thereof on the part of the preparatory committee."

Any hope that the declaration might be approved by the conference without amendment — as something no one was completely happy with but everyone could live with — was shattered on the opening day. The Chinese, only recently admitted to the U.N., made it plain even before delegates from all nations had completed registration that they wanted the draft reopened for discussion. Morale among those delegates who had worked for a strong declaration immediately plummeted: it was felt that once the document was opened for amendment by one nation, a whole avalanche of amendments from other unsatisfied delegations would inevitably descend. Were that to happen, it seemed extremely unlikely that any new draft, agreeable to all nations present, could be pieced together in the short time available at the conference. The prospects became even gloomier when a number of nations, including Australia, India and Nigeria, jumped on the Chinese bandwagon, indicating that they too had amendments to propose. (In the end a total of 47 amendments were proposed; most were later withdrawn.) To make matters worse, no one could be sure they understood the Chinese motives in asking that the declaration be opened up for discussion. That nation had been out of the mainstream of world diplomacy for so long that almost no one had experience in dealing with its diplomats. It was all very well for the Chinese to say that they wanted an opportunity to discuss the declaration because they had not been members of the U.N. during most of the time it was being drafted, and had therefore not been able to play a role in the work of the I.W.G. — but was that the real reason behind their actions?

To try to head off the looming crisis, the Swedish host delegation sponsored informal consultations at the Swedish foreign office over the next two days. During those discussions the Chinese remained consistent in their position that their attitude to the declaration was "positive", but that they felt that the "democratic" thing to do was to allow full discussion of it. As a compromise Canada suggested that an informal, open-ended working group be set up with the understanding that nations would avoid presenting formal amendments, but rather deposit their disagreements in oral or written statements of position to be read into the conference record during the closing plenary session. It was a well-worn expedient, recognized in international law as affording protection to the objecting nation. However, by the end of the first day no agreement had been reached. The French, who had been opposed, like most other European nations, to the inclusion of legal precepts, made it plain at that time that they were prepared to surrender any hope of agreement on the 23 principles in the declaration and settle for acceptance by the conference of the preamble alone. Earlier in the day they had passed the U.S. delegation a paper outlining certain written exchanges with the Chinese which, they said, showed that the Chinese held strong views on the need for major alterations in the declaration. On the basis of this information the U.S. delegate informed the Canadians that it was "quite clear" that the Chinese were "out to wreck the declaration". Canada, however, unlike most other industrialized nations present, had been carefully nurturing contacts with the Chinese for several years, and had in the months before the conference made a point of keeping the Chinese informed of its position on a number of environmental questions. From these contacts Canada had been able to arrive at some conclusions, however sketchy, about Chinese intentions. Armed with their impressions, Canadian delegates argued with the Americans that the Peking position was equally consistent with simply wanting to be heard and make some sort of constructive contribution. They pointed out the Chinese had repeatedly stated in private contact that they wanted to see the declaration adopted by consensus at the conference.

As the foreign-office negotiations got under way on the second day, there was general agreement on setting up a working group along lines proposed at the previous meeting. Once this had become clear, the Chinese delegate left the meeting, drove to the *Folkets Hus* where the plenary session was droning on through opening statements by the various nations, and asked to be heard. He then co-opted the work of the foreign-office negotiating group by proposing to the plenary session that an ad-hoc committee be set up to examine the draft declaration. The other nations involved in the negotiations were caught flat-footed, and had to scramble to take part in the brief plenary debate that followed. It was not a complete *coup* for the Chinese, however. Several African nations, whose small delegations were already being stretched to the limit trying to attend all the existing committee meetings, argued strongly for a small, closed committee in which they would be able to insist on proportional representation. The Chinese were put in the embarrassing position of arguing against the Africans and in favour of a more "democratic", open-ended, working group. At the end this position prevailed, largely in deference to the argument that the debate over who should sit on any closed committee could very well occupy all the time remaining for the conference.

The working group held a total of 15 closed meetings from June 9 to 15, many of which stretched into the early hours of the morning. The key officers of the group were chairman Taieb Slim, Secretary of State of Tunisia, and rapporteur T. C. Bacon of Canada. The roles played by these two men proved, in different ways, crucial to the outcome of the committee's deliberations. Discussion got off to a rocky start, and under Slim's inflexible chairmanship seemed to bounce from one near-disaster to another as days dragged by and delegates' tempers wore thinner and thinner. Slim angered many delegates on the first morning by demonstrating what seemed to be a lack of awareness of the crucial nature of the discussions or of the critical shortage of time by giving no opportunity to China, or any other nation that had not taken part in the deliberations of the I.W.G. to be heard. Instead, he allowed a long, sterile and acrimonious debate between Brazil and Argentina over the question of states' duties to consult with neighbours likely to be affected by projects of environmental impact. Brazil, needless to say, was opposed to the inclusion of the principle, while Argentina wanted it strengthened. In the afternoon, however, the Chinese

were finally given a chance to state their position, and caused something of a sensation by presenting the committee with a ten-point statement. These were immediately interpreted by many delegates as
proposed amendments to the draft declaration and once again gloom
prevailed, since it was clear that several of the proposals were unacceptable to the U.S. and other western nations. Again, however, the
Chinese took the trouble to meet privately with the Canadian delegates to make it clear that this was not the case — that they simply
wanted their proposals fully discussed. They reinforced this point by
leaking the ten-point plan to the press through a reporter working for
the Stockholm conference *Eco*, a daily tabloid newspaper operated
jointly by the Friends of Earth and *The Ecologist* magazine. It was
among the first major Chinese interventions in an international forum
since the Communist revolution in that country, and as such was a
document of some significance.

1) RELATIONSHIP BETWEEN ECONOMIC DEVELOPMENT AND ENVIRONMENT

Economic development and social progress are necessary for the
welfare of mankind and the further improvement of the environment. The developing countries want to build a modern industry
and agriculture to safeguard their national independence and
assure their development. A distinction must be made between
these countries and a few highly developed countries. The environmental policies of each nation must not impede development.

2) POPULATION GROWTH AND ENVIRONMENTAL PROTECTION

Man is the most precious of all things on Earth. Man propels
social progress, creates social wealth and advances science and
technology. There are no grounds for any pessimistic views on
population growth and the preservation of the environment. Both
can be solved by national policies: the control of urban population, settlement in agricultural areas, publicity for the environment, advocation of family planning, etc.

3) SOCIAL ROOT CAUSE OF ENVIRONMENTAL POLLUTION

We hold that the major social root cause of environmental pollution is capitalism, which has developed into a state of imperialism,
monopoly, colonialism and neocolonialism — seeking high profits,
not concerned with the life or death of people, and discharging
poisons at will. It is the policies of the super powers that have
resulted in the most serious harm to the environment. The United
States has committed serious abuses in Vietnam, killing and
wounding many of its inhabitants. These facts are known to the

world and should be included in the declaration. The declaration should also be comprehensive on the nuclear threat.

4) PROTECTION OF RESOURCES

Every country should be entitled to utilize and to exploit its resources for its own needs. We resolutely oppose the plundering of resources in the developing countries by the highly developed countries.

5) STRUGGLE AGAINST POLLUTION

The governments of all countries must take steps to prevent the discharge of pollutants into the environment. We support the people in all countries who are struggling against pollution.

6) INTERNATIONAL POLLUTION COMPENSATION

Each country has the right to safeguard its environment. The corporate states are discharging pollutants and the victim states have a right to compensation.

7) INTERNATIONAL EXCHANGE OF SCIENCE AND TECHNOLOGY

All countries should actively employ science and technology to safeguard the environment. Science and technology should not be monopolized by one or two countries. They must be available for the protection of the environment in the developing countries.

8) VOLUNTARY FUND

The creation and management of an environmental fund has been proposed. The principal industrialized countries and the most serious polluters should make the contributions to this fund.

9) WORLD ENVIRONMENTAL BODY

The intergovernmental body which has been proposed to guide and direct environmental policy must respect the sovereignty of all countries. This body must be free from control by the super powers.

10) INTERNATIONAL ENVIRONMENTAL PROTECTION AND STATE SOVEREIGNTY

Any international agreement should respect the sovereignty of all countries. No country should encroach on another under the pretext of environmental protection.

While the initial reaction to the Chinese statement had been one of pessimism, it quickly became clear to a number of delegations that once the document was stripped of its florid prose and irritating but unimportant irrelevancies, it did not differ in any significant respect from the position taken in the official conference working papers. In some ways it was remarkably similar to the Canadian draft declaration — in fact, the Canadians found themselves with an unexpected ally in their demands that the declaration retain the legal principles of responsibility not to pollute (no. 5 of the Chinese statement), compensation (no. 6) and consultation (covered in part by no. 7). Once the wake left by the Chinese statement had settled, discussions proceeded relatively smoothly, with the exception of the constant threat of polarization between the developed and developing nations. Whenever Chinese delegates felt their position was being ignored, they took the floor to make strong statements attacking colonialism, imperialism and capitalism, themes which would then be taken up by one or more of the other developing nations.

These effective little reminders of the potential strength of the Chinese delegation invariably stopped short of anything that could be interpreted as direct threat or coercion. For the most part, moreover, the Chinese indulged in generalities only infrequently, and though their statements were normally couched in Maoist rhetoric, most of them stuck to specific principles. The Americans, for their part, confined their comments on the Chinese position to brief, caustic interjections: their attitude caused at least one Western participant to question, in an official communication with his government, whether the U.S. was not pursuing the same tactic it had accused the Chinese of adopting — that is, paying lip service to the declaration in order to mask a real desire to destroy it. Further difficulties were caused by destructively prima-donna-like behaviour on the part of delegates from Iran, India, Uruguay, Egypt and Sweden, all of whom seemed more interested in the role of leader than in the direction in which the group was being led. Some of the more constructive effort was provided by delegates from Ceylon, Cameroun, Canada, Mexico, Finland, Britain, New Zealand, Pakistan and Japan. The difference in the performance of these delegates was a bleak reminder of the crucial role personal idiosyncrasies can play in the most important of international gatherings.

The committee had just wound up the first half of its third day of discussion when chairman Slim dropped a new bombshell: he announced that afternoon's (Saturday's) meeting would be cancelled, as would the meeting planned for Sunday. He insisted, instead, on setting up a small drafting group confined to those nations that had sponsored formal amendments. This included the Americans, who had taken the precaution of proposing a token amendment, but not the Chinese, who had complied with calls for restraint in tampering with the draft declaration and refrained from proposing formal amendments. For once the usually impassive Chinese diplomats displayed real anger. They felt that they were being relegated to the role of observers, and there was once again a real danger of a complete breakdown in negotiation. The day was saved only by a hastily-arranged working dinner at which a number of nations made it clear to the Chinese that they too were frustrated and unhappy with Slim's leadership.

As the discussion reconvened the following Monday, several delegations began making serious efforts to extract the essential meaning from the Chinese proposals and discuss them on this basis. A novel technique was being used in the attempt to avoid rich-poor polarization and skirt nationalist sensitivities: nations that felt they had constructive proposals to make met in small groups in the lobby outside the meeting room, or in corners of the room itself, to draft brief papers which would then be presented anonymously for discussion to the larger group, usually through a delegate from a relatively uninvolved nation. They were drawn up deliberately with a view to preserving the original draft while adding the ideas of the Chinese and Africans. Canada was able to play a leading role in organizing this system by virtue of the fact that one of its representatives was the committee rapporteur, and in a position to know the views of most of the participating nations as well as those of the conference secretariat. To conceal Bacon's dual role and avoid any flare-up over conflict-of-interest charges, the Canadians submitted their proposals through the Iranian delegate, who clearly enjoyed playing the statesman. The device nearly backfired in an amusing, if hair-raising, sort of way when the Iranian, inflated by his role of apparent stewardship, accepted an Indian invitation to help organize a large group of the developing nations behind a plan to give up on the negotiations and forward the draft declaration to the next meeting of the U.N. assembly. The Canadians got wind of the plan at the last possible moment, and succeeded in scotching it by persuading the Iranian that he was the only person who could hold the working group together by feeding the "anonymous" proposals into the mill. Its leadership split, the Indian plan dissolved before it could reach the floor.

Heartening progress was being made with the device of the anonymous proposals when the committee's work was again disrupted by an ill-timed intervention by Maurice Strong, who convened a parallel meeting of the heads of all delegations to try to break the "deadlock" on the key areas of colonialism, economic questions and nuclear testing.

In fact, the working group had already found an acceptable approach to the first two issues, and in the event, the third was never to be satisfactorily resolved. However, the chairman decided to adjourn the working group, which was already dangerously short of time, until Strong's group had concluded its meeting. The high-level talks went on for several hours, but at last simply turned the whole debate over once again to the working group. Only on the issue of nuclear weapons did it have a concrete proposal to make.

By the evening of the seventh day of negotiation, most delegates were clearly in the final stages of exhaustion. Only the fact that this was their last chance to salvage the important declaration kept them working feverishly. While their exhaustion seemed to exude a kind of creative tension, it meant also that a good idea often went unrecognized. In its last edition the *Eco* summed up:

> As the *Eco* goes to press it is overwhelmingly probable that a draft declaration will be finalized this evening. Or that it will not. This is the unanimous opinion of those privy to the deliberations now taking place. A spokesman for the Asian group of delegations put it this way: "We *must* agree on a declaration here at Stockholm. If it goes to New York it will be even worse." A highly-placed source — who endorses this description of himself — said late Thursday that there was simply no question about it: a text would be agreed before the end of the evening. He drew upon 25 years of U.N. experience to point out that this is the usual way of transacting business: irreconcilable disagreement to the last minute, and then, out of the chaos, consensus. A member of the secretariat emerging moments later from the inner sanctum behind the billowing curtains, shook his head solemnly. "They are still discussing principle 19," he lamented. "At least four more principles to go — plus the preamble. It's impossible." A Chinese delegate clutching a red book ducked into a telephone booth. Shortly thereafter principle 19 was set aside and the working group moved on to principle 20. Shortly thereafter principle 20 was set aside and the working group moved on to principle 21.

This is not to suggest that principles 1 through 18 had achieved unquestioning acceptance. Disputation ranged freely through the thickening sheaf of working papers. Impromptu press conferences coalesced and dispersed. Every time a pink rectangle (delegates' badges were pink) appeared through the curtains hung across the meeting-room entrance, the hungry journalists converged like vultures. They derived little sustenance. Christian Herter, leader of the U.S. delegation, accosted outside the curtains by an *Eco* reporter, offered an apt if inadvertent summary: "I don't know anything, so don't ask me."

In fact, the eleventh-hour negotiations had been even more dramatic than the *Eco* had supposed. The final — and most sensational — crisis faced by the committee blew up over some particularly inept handling by the chairman of the principle of the draft declaration that dealt with nuclear testing. Pushing it through the working group, Slim announced suddenly that consensus had been achieved. The Chinese promptly intervened to state that they did not agree with the principle: earlier in the evening the Brazilians had succeeded in having the article dealing with consultation tabled, to be dealt with by the U.N. General Assembly, and the Chinese expected equal treatment on the nuclear-arms issue. They and their supporters wanted the declaration to call for "the complete prohibition and thorough destruction of nuclear weapons". The U.S. and its supporters wanted it to call for a stop to nuclear testing in the atmosphere alone. The proposal the Chinese found unacceptable stated: "Man and his environment must be spared the effects of nuclear weapons and all other means of mass destruction. States must strive to reach prompt agreement, in the relevant international organs, on the elimination and complete destruction of such weapons."[1]

Chairman Slim chose to ignore the Chinese intervention and again announced consensus. Again the Chinese delegate objected, and again Slim ignored him. The argument continued for nearly fifteen minutes, with the Chinese becoming increasingly more isolated and humiliated. The Americans seemed extremely pleased, and began approaching other delegates to tell them that the Chinese were intent on wrecking the declaration, that the situation was hopeless, and that the entire matter should be referred to the General Assembly. The Canadians, seeing disaster looming ever larger, frantically contacted Maurice Strong and asked him to intervene to try to persuade Slim to adjourn the meeting briefly to allow tempers to cool. Strong agreed, but Slim refused. Secretly, Strong then ordered an aide to unplug the interpreting device. Faced with a gap in simultaneous translation, Slim had no choice but to adjourn while "repairs" were effected, thus making possible informal discussion among delegates on how to proceed.

In the end, the Chinese allowed the nuclear-arms principle to remain in the draft, electing to make their objections public by not taking part in the vote on the declaration at the final conference plenary session that morning and by making a brief speech stating their position. Thus the chairman of the plenary was able to avoid a vote and announce that the declaration as a whole had been adopted by consensus. The Chinese statement of position amounted simply to a re-reading of part of their original speech to the plenary.

> We deem it necessary here for us to say a few words on the question of nuclear monopoly, nuclear threats and nuclear blackmail by the superpowers. The superpowers are vigorously developing their nuclear weapons and stepping up their nuclear-arms race in their struggle for hegemony. They have not only manufactured and stockpiled large quantities of nuclear weapons within their own countries, but have also set up nuclear bases on the territory of other countries, thus constituting a great threat to the human environment and the security of the people of the world. For the purpose of safeguarding international peace, protecting the security and environment of mankind, a resolute struggle must be waged against the nuclear monopoly, nuclear threats and nuclear blackmail of the superpowers.
>
> China develops nuclear weapons solely for the purpose of defence and for breaking the nuclear monopoly and ultimately eliminating nuclear weapons and nuclear war. China's nuclear weapons are still in the experimental stage. The Chinese government has consistently stood for the complete prohibition and thorough destruction of nuclear weapons and proposed to convene a summit conference of all countries of the world to discuss this question and, as a first step, to reach an agreement on the non-use of nuclear weapons at no time and under no circumstances [sic]. Our government has on many occasions declared that at no time and under no circumstances will China be the first to use nuclear weapons. However, the superpowers which possess large quantities of nuclear weapons have to this date refused to commit themselves not to be the first to use nuclear weapons. For this, all the countries and people who cherish peace and uphold justice cannot but express their utmost indignation.
>
> At present there are some countries which are worried by nuclear pollution. Such sentiment is understandable. But we hold that the fundamental cause of the threat to the existence of mankind and the human environment by nuclear war should be eliminated. It is regrettable that there are now certain people who ignore the fact that the superpowers have manufactured and stockpiled large quantities of nuclear weapons and threaten the small and medium countries. They ignore the fact that the U.S. government is conducting a barbarous war in Vietnam, Laos and Cambodia, massacring the people and poisoning the environment. On the contrary, they pretend to be impartial and oppose all nuclear tests without making any distinction. This is what the Chinese oppose.

As with actions taken by all international conferences of this type, the principles contained in the declaration carried weight only in so far as they had been accepted by a large majority of the nations of the world. To the extent that states voiced their disagreement with them, the authority of the principles was diminished. For the Canadian government, at least, the key principles represented important statements of international environmental law. In order to have this belief clearly on the record and thereby shore up the authority of the declaration Alan Beesley, the delegation's legal advisor and chief negotiator, made the following brief statement of interpretation following acceptance of the document by plenary.

The Canadian government considers that principle 21 (formerly 18) reflects customary international law in affirming the principle that states have, in accordance with the Charter of the United Nations and the principles of international law, "the sovereign right to exploit their own resources pursuant to their own environmental policies, and the responsibility to ensure that activities within their jurisdiction or control do not cause damage to the environment of other states or of areas beyond the limits of national jurisdiction."

The Canadian government considers that the secondary consequential principle 22 (formerly 19) reflects an existing duty of states when it proclaims the principle that "the states should co-operate to develop further the international law regarding liability and compensation for the victims of pollution and other environmental damage caused by activities within the jurisdiction or control of such states to areas beyond their jurisdiction."

The Canadian government considers also that the tertiary consequential principle contained in the draft declaration on the human environment as it first came before us in plenary (former principle 20 not now contained in the draft) on the duty of states to inform one another considering the environmental impact of their actions upon areas beyond their jurisdiction also reflected a duty under existing customary international law, when it proclaimed, in essence, the principle "that relevant information must be supplied by states on activities or developments within their jurisdiction or under their control whenever there is reason to believe that such information is needed to avoid the risk of significant adverse effects on the environment in areas beyond their national jurisdiction."

These principles, taken together with the important and closely-related marine pollution principles and the draft articles on a proposed dumping convention, on which we have already taken action, together provide us with an opportunity to work together in a co-operative spirit of conciliation and accommodation (accommodation not only as between differing national interests but as between national interests and the interests of the international community) to elaborate laws that will protect us all by protecting our environment.

The U.S., to its credit, tried hard in its end-of-conference statement to make the best of what amounted to a series of defeats, but mentioned only one of the three important legal principles.

> The final text [of the declaration], although uneven in the view of the United States delegation, preserves a number of extremely important principles of conduct for states in dealing with environmental problems of international significance. Chief among these is principle 21, which declares that states have "the responsibility to ensure that activities within their jurisdiction or control do not cause damage to the environment of other states or of areas beyond the limits of national jurisdiction". Also of notable importance are such provisions as principle 2, declaring that the earth's living and non-living resources, and representative samples of natural ecosystems, must be safeguarded for present and future generations; principle 6 stating that excessive discharge of toxic substances and heat into the environment must be halted to prevent "serious or irreversible damage" to ecosystems; principle 16 calling for application of appropriate demographic policies where growth rates or concentration of population are likely to have adverse effects on the environment or on development; and principle 25, declaring the obligation of states to "ensure that international organizations play a co-ordinated efficient and dynamic role for the protection and improvement of the environment".

For a U.S. delegation that had arrived in Stockholm with White House instructions to get "a headline a day", the battle over the declaration seemed to have been a sobering experience. To put it crudely, the conference had turned out to be something more than the public-relations festival they had apparently been counting on. They had not, of course, been alone in their hopes: most other major industrial powers would also have preferred to see less substantive action. If it can be said that international law is habitually developed by the weaker nations to protect their interests from the stronger nations (who can look after themselves), Stockholm was proving to be no exception to the rule.

NOTE

1. A related resolution which called upon "those states intending to carry out nuclear weapons tests (particularly in the atmosphere) to abandon their plans to carry out such tests as they may lead to further contamination of the environment," was drafted in committee III (pollution and organizational matters). Proposed jointly by New Zealand and Peru — and aimed specifically at France and China, neither of whom has signed the test-ban treaty — it was approved in plenary by the conference over the objections of France, China and Gabon.

Much Pollution Work for China, Official Says

STOCKHOLM *(Staff) — With Soviet bloc countries absent from the U.N. environmental conference, a good deal of attention has been focused on the 31-man Chinese delegation. At all parallel conferences being run by an assortment of groups, some including academics of international repute such as Margaret Mead, reference constantly is made to China's efforts to solve its pollution problems.*

But one of the Chinese delegation's leaders, Ho Hsiang-lin of Peking's Institute of Petroleum, insists China still has much work to do. Three years ago, he said, the government set up a special department of pollution under the State Planning Commission. It has responsibility for deciding the location of and pollution control for most new factories, including refineries, chemical plants and textile and steel mills.

"Pollution standards on existing factories also come under the new department rather than local revolutionary committees," he said. The Chinese delegation has not formulated positions on all conference subjects, Ho said, because it has received Chinese translations only recently from the U.N. "We still have not got the proposed declaration of the conference translated completely and several of our delegation members can read only Chinese." . . .

Last night, the Chinese delegation attended a meeting of Asian countries. So far, China has played a low-key role in U.N. affairs. A matter of acute interest is whether the Chinese will take a leadership role at this conference, with the East bloc countries absent and with considerable pressure from underdeveloped countries to force poverty and colonization on the agenda as logical environmental problems.

The Globe and Mail (Toronto), June 6, 1972

Chapter six

Towards a new law of the environment

Just as mounting evidence of the terrible impact of man-made pollution had for ever destroyed the romantic notion of "the boundless and everlasting oceans", the Stockholm conference was to play its part in laying to rest the millenia-old concept of freedom of the high seas. In fact, the second blow to our naivety was demanded by the first: if respected scientists the world over were warning that the life-giving marine biosystems might soon be damaged beyond repair by oil, pesticides, pcbs, and other toxic effluents, it was clear action was essential to bring about rational management of the sea. That meant, among other things, enforced regulation of conduct on the high seas. Once it was realized that all states — shipowning or not — had a vested interest in the continuing health and productivity of the oceans, the age-old legal principles which gave flag states sole jurisdiction over the conduct of their merchant fleets became untenable. Coastal states in particular, their coastlines vulnerable to deliberate and accidental discharges of harmful materials, had begun to demand a bigger role in regulating use of the vast common of the seas.

Although a number of international accords regulating behaviour on the high seas in limited and specific ways had been signed in recent years as a result of the growing threat of pollution,[1] it was not until Stockholm that generalized limitations to freedom of the high seas were endorsed by a broadly representative gathering of the nations of the world. Principles 7 and 21 of the Declaration on the Human Environment touched on this important area. By far the most significant advances were made, however, with the conference's acceptance of the Statement of Objectives and Principles on the Marine Environment elaborated by the 41 nations of the intergovernmental working group on marine pollution set up by the conference preparatory committee. Meeting in Ottawa early in November, 1971, the group formulated its statement:

> The marine environment and all the living organisms which it supports are of vital importance to humanity and all people have an interest in assuring that this environment is so managed that its quality and resources are not impaired. This applies especially to coastal nations, which have a particular interest in the man-

agement of coastal area resources. The capacity of the sea to assimi-
late wastes and render them harmless and its ability to regenerate
natural resources is not unlimited. Proper management is required and measures to prevent and control marine pollution must
be regarded as an essential element in this management of the
oceans and seas and their natural resources.

In the view of the Canadian government, at least as expressed in a
working paper prepared for the 1972 summer session of the U.N.'s Sea-
bed Committee,

> the importance of this statement cannot be overemphasized. With
> respect to marine pollution, existing law is based on laissez-faire
> concepts and does not recognize the need for regulation based on
> scientific principles. The Statement of Objectives, on the other
> hand, recognizes that there are limits to the assimilative and re-
> generative capacities of the sea and the inevitable consequential
> conclusion that it is necessary to apply management concepts to
> the marine environment, to marine resources and to the preserva-
> tion of the marine environment.

Management techniques, of course, would mean an end to freedom
of the high seas. The 23 principles that followed the statement were
designed to provide a comprehensive framework within which rational
management could take place. They ranged from a general statement of
states' "duty to protect and preserve the marine environment" to the
need for a comprehensive marine pollution monitoring system and the
establishment of national and international regulations to curb pollution. The principles also dealt with enforcement of regulations, calling
on all states to ensure that their ships comply with internationally-
recognized rules and standards, and that their national legislation
"provides adequate sanctions against those who infringe existing regulations on marine pollution". Coastal states were authorized to intervene in cases of accidents on the high seas which posed a pollution
threat to their coastline "and to take appropriate measures as may be
necessary to prevent, mitigate, or eliminate such danger. . ."

Three further principles which would greatly increase the jurisdiction of coastal states over neighbouring waters were fiercely debated
at the Ottawa meeting, to be passed on to Stockholm eventually as a
kind of minority report endorsed by 20 small and middle powers. They
had been drafted by Canada, possessor of the world's longest coastline
and thus a natural leader in the battle to whittle down the absolute
authority of flag nations over ocean shipping. Vigorously opposing the
Canadian position were the big shipping nations, including most of
the west European countries, Greece, the U.K., U.S.A. and U.S.S.R.

The first of the three principles stated that "a state may exercise special authority in areas of the sea adjacent to its territorial waters where functional controls of a continuing nature are necessary for the effective prevention of pollution which could cause damage or injury to the land or marine environment under its exclusive or sovereign authority." In practical terms, this would give coastal states the right to ensure that ships coming within 50 to 100 miles of its shores or perhaps even 200 miles (depending on the coastal state concerned) complied with international or special local anti-pollution regulations. (A similar law aimed at protecting the fragile Arctic environment was recently passed unilaterally by the Canadian parliament.) The second of the three principles would give a coastal state the right to prohibit vessels not complying with international or local anti-pollution regulations from sailing in "waters under its environmental protection authority". (Again, this would range from 50 to 100 miles out or even 200 miles out, depending on the extent of claims to jurisdiction of the nation concerned. It was expected that future Law of the Sea conferences would draft agreements which would define "jurisdiction" more clearly.) The third principle outlined the basis for coastal states' authority:

> The basis on which a state should exercise rights or powers, in addition to its sovereign rights or powers, pursuant to its special authority in areas adjacent to its territorial waters, is that such rights or powers should be deemed to be delegated to that state by the world community on behalf of humanity as a whole. The rights and powers exercised must be consistent with the coastal state's primary responsibility for marine environmental protection in the areas concerned: they should be subject to international rules and standards and to review before an appropriate international tribunal.

So far-reaching were these proposals that the Canadian delegation to the working group could hardly have expected acquiescence from the flag states. Neither, however, were they prepared for the kinds of tactics used in the attempt to keep them off the Stockholm agenda. During the first two days of the meeting in Ottawa, developing nations were to grow increasingly frustrated as the Norwegian, Danish and Italian chairmen of the three working-group subcommittees consistently headed off attempts to have the marine principles discussed. Finally, the Kenyan delegation threatened to walk out of the meeting and take with it as many other developing nations as possible unless more time was devoted to the principles. The threat worked, but in the closing hours of the conference, the developing nations became angered again as Norwegian chairman Jens Boyesen blocked the attempt to include a direct reference in the conference report to the fact that the three Canadian principles had been actively supported by 20 of the 41 nations in attendance. The matter was settled to the satisfaction of the developing nations three times, but each time the chairman allowed the question to be re-opened by one of the European shipping states. In the end it was firmly agreed to list the three controversial principles separately in the report along with a list of the nations supporting them. When the French version of the report was issued (the first language to be printed), no such information could be found. Instead, the report listed several Spanish proposals and noted that a number of delegations had supported them. This was not, in fact, the case. As the Spanish delegate was to point out later during debate, there had been no time for the conference to even discuss his country's proposals. The Canadians were in the dark as to what had happened until a member of their delegation overheard the chairman of the subcommittee which had debated the marine principles urging Boyesen to "reconsider" his position on the inclusion of the three principles in the conference report: the delegate drew the obvious conclusion. The English version of the report, which came out much later, did take note of the three principles, but did not list the names of supporting nations as agreed.

The small and middle powers were to score another significant victory at the Ottawa conference during discussion of a proposed ocean dumping accord. As originally proposed by the U.S., with the support of Britain and most other European shipping nations, the dumping agreement would have been limited to a system of permits administered by each state within its own jurisdiction; it was left to the coastal states to decide when and what to dump in waters under their jurisdiction and there was no provision made for enforcement or establishing liability. Canada, Mexico, Spain, and several other delegations considered this merely a licence to dump, and fought, successfully, for a much tougher agreement. The final draft was to include a "black list" naming materials that states would not be allowed to dump in the oceans in any circumstances and a "grey list" of materials that could be dumped only after consideration had been given by an appropriate international body (under U.N. supervision) to "the possible persistence or permanence of the effects of the proposed dumping, the volume, concentration and toxicity of materials and substances involved, the geographic position ... (including the depth of water, distance from the nearest coast and the distance from fishing grounds and amenity areas) the characteristics of the location in relation to decomposition and dispersal of materials and in relation to exploitable resources ..." Included in the black list (dumping prohibited) were mercury, cadmium, organohalogen compounds — including Aldrin, Lindane, Chlordane, DDT, Dieldrin, Heptachlor, Hexachlorobenzene, polyhalogenated biphenyls and Toxaphene — with oil and derivative hydrocarbons, plastics and other persistent synthetic materials, biological and chemical warfare agents and high-level radioactive wastes. The grey list included low-level radioactive wastes, arsenic, lead, copper and zinc and their compounds, organosilicon compounds, cyanides and fluorides, pesticides not covered in the black list and acids containing any of the above materials and/or beryllium, chromium, nickel or vanadium. (At the insistence of the U.S., military vessels were exempted from the agreement.)

Both the dumping accord and the marine pollution principles were dealt with by committee III (pollution and organizational matters) at Stockholm, the dumping agreement having arrived there by way of another international conference held in Reykjavik in April of 1972 where the document was further refined. There had been some early hope that it might be signed into international law at Stockholm, but it soon became clear that several nations wanted more time to study it before committing their governments. The committee eventually agreed to forward the document to the U.N. Committee on the Peaceful Uses of the Sea-Bed and the Ocean Floor Beyond the Limits of National Jurisdiction for comment, and on from there to a U.N.-sponsored convention to be held in London before the end of 1972, where it would be opened for signature.[2]

For the 23 marine pollution principles and the tag-along Canadian principles giving new authority to the coastal states, the going in committee III was considerably rougher. To begin with, the controversial Canadian principles had once again disappeared mysteriously somewhere between Ottawa — where it had been agreed to forward them with neither approval nor rejection from the working group — and Stockholm. They were not included in the preparatory committee's working paper on identification and control of pollutants. To the increasing irritation of the U.S. and British delegations, Canada once again insisted that the three principles be inserted in the document. The revised working paper thus stated that the nations attending the Stockholm conference "take note of the principles ... and refer [them] to the 1973 Law of the Sea Conference for such action as may be appropriate". The other 23 principles were to be "collectively endorsed as a basis for general agreement" and referred to the 1973 conferences of the Intergovernmental Marine Consultative Organization and the Law of the Sea group. During the committee debate the U.S. proposed that the working paper be amended so that the 23 principles would simply be forwarded without Stockholm's endorsement. After running into stiff opposition from the smaller powers, who had been joined in their battle by China, the Americans withdrew their amendment in favour of a British amendment which called upon the two 1973 conferences to "give careful consideration" to the principles. That amendment was defeated by a vote of 20 for, 25 against, and seven abstentions. The committee then approved, by 32–13–9, a Canadian amendment (co-sponsored by Ghana, Iceland, Mexico and Spain) according to which governments agreed to "collectively endorse" the 23 principles as "guiding concepts" for the two legal conventions. The final vote on the endorsement and forwarding all 26 principles, taken together, was about as close as it could be, and was not taken before the large seafaring nations had been defeated in a last-ditch attempt for adjournment of the committee meeting to give them time to consolidate their support. The recommendations were to pass by a single vote. Following plenary-session endorsement of the committee's decision, both the U.S. and Japan made statements explaining that they had been among those voting against the endorsement of the principles because they felt the two 1973 legal conferences were the only proper forums for such legal questions.

By an ironic twist of fate, at least one of the legal principles endorsed at Stockholm was to be tested for the first time just two weeks after the conference had ended. On June 8, the third day of the conference, the Canadian delegation to Stockholm received the following telegram from Ottawa:

FM EXTOTT FPR160 JUN 8/72
TO WSHDC FLASH . . . . STKHM/MIN DAVIS DELIVER BY 090800
—Oil spill incident at Cherry Point.
Following is statement made in House of Commons by SSEA [Secretary of State for External Affairs] June 7: "On Sunday, June 4, the tanker *World Bond* discharged approximately 12,000 gallons of crude oil into the sea while engaged in unloading operations at the Atlantic Richfield refinery at Cherry Point, which is just south of the Canada-U.S. boundary in the state of Washington. Some of this oil quickly spread into Canadian waters. The incident at Cherry Point is a stark reminder of what we have stated on many occasions: that far more serious spills will inevitably take place on other occasions if oil is moved by tanker through the Strait of Juan

de Fuca. It demonstrates that in the event of a spill on the U.S. side, damage will almost certainly be suffered in Canada, and this damage could be severe. Even the small quantity of oil which escaped on this occasion moved rapidly northward across the boundary and collected on some five miles of one of the finest beaches in the area.

"We have, of course, registered with the U.S.A. Canada's grave concern about this ominous incident. On instructions, our embassy yesterday emphasized to the State Department that the incident confirmed our anxieties over the threat to the ecology and resources of this inland marine area from oil tankers. The embassy made clear that the Canadian government expects full and prompt compensation for all damages suffered in Canada, as well as full clean-up costs, to be paid by those responsible. The embassy restated our broad concerns about the hazards which will arise from the movement by tanker of large quantities of oil into the Cherry Point refineries (once oil starts flowing from the Alaskan north slope fields). We have made repeated representations to the U.S.A. government about the proposed increase in oil tanker traffic into this area, and indeed we raised this matter with President Nixon when he visited Canada in mid-April. . . . We are especially concerned to ensure observance of the principle established in the 1938 Trail Smelter arbitration between Canada and the U.S.A. This has established that one country may not permit the use of its territory in such a manner as to cause injury to the territory of another and shall be responsible to pay compensation for any injury so suffered. Canada accepted this responsibility in the Trail smelter case (in which effluent from a smelter in Canada damaged property in the U.S.A.) and we would expect that the same principle would be implemented in the present situation. Indeed, this principle has already received acceptance by a considerable number of states and hopefully it will be adopted at the Stockholm conference as a fundamental rule of international environmental law. . ."

The Canadian government supported its embassy's representations to the U.S. State Department with a three-page *aide-mémoire* in which it reminded Washington that "during negotiations on the declaration on the human environment, the United States gave full and unqualified support to the inclusion in the declaration of the principle of state responsibility for activities within its jurisdiction against extraterritorial damage. During the preparatory process leading to that declaration, the United States representative alluded to this principle as a 'legal norm' upon which states should base their activities." The Canadian government, for its part, considered that "principle 21 of the declaration reflects customary international law in affirming that states have, in accordance with the Charter of the United Nations and the principles of international law, the sovereign right to exploit their own resources pursuant to their own environmental policies and the responsibility to ensure that activities within their jurisdiction or control do not cause damage to the environment of other states or of areas beyond the limits of national jurisdiction." The diplomatic note concluded:

> In the view of Canadian authorities, the best way of proceeding in this case is to divorce the question of liability from possible obligations of compensation. Thus, whoever may in the end pay for the costs of clean-up and/or damage to the property of the Canadian government, such issues need not hold up the determination of liability. Whether or not Atlantic Richfield accepts liability in whole or in part, it is important in the view of the Canadian government to make known to the Canadian public as soon as possible that the United States accepts ultimate liability for this type of incident.
> In the circumstances, the question of liability or damage arising from the Cherry Point spill could be resolved through a simple application of principle 21 which has been drawn from the principle embodied in the decision of the Trail Smelter arbitration.

The American reply to the *aide-mémoire* was cautiously circuitous — almost ludicrously so — but it accepted nonetheless the authority of principle 21:

> The U.S. government continues to give full support to principle 21 of the declaration on the human environment as well as to the principle enunciated in the Trail Smelter arbitration. Although the declaration generally is a statement of moral responsibility and obligation, in so far as principle 21 is consistent with customary international law and widely accepted treaty obligations, the U.S.A. regards it as declaratory of international law. In this connection, the U.S.A. calls attention to principle 22 of the declaration, supported by both the U.S.A. and Canadian governments, which reads: "States shall co-operate to develop further the international law regarding liability and compensation for the victims of pollution and other environmental damage caused by activities within the jurisdiction or control of such states to areas beyond their jurisdiction."

Having already accepted the authority of principle 21, the U.S. note backtracked to add:

> The U.S.A. believes that the action called for by principle 22 is necessary to render principle 21 an effective and usable deterrent to transnational environmental damage. ... Accordingly, it is the view of the U.S.A. that, in light of the actions of Atlantic Richfield in [promising to honour] all claims arising out of the Cherry Point spill, the primary interest of claimants, public and private,

in receiving prompt compensation will be best served by permit-
ting settlement to proceed without introducing the difficult and
unsettled questions of law and policy which are unavoidably
raised in the refinement of principle 21. The U.S.A. is interested,
nevertheless, in the views of Canada on how the refinement of
principle 21, as well as principle 22, ought to proceed . . .

If the American note did nothing else, it defined the phrase *"circular
caveat"* for all time. Nevertheless, the Canadian government has chosen
to interpret the note as a further strengthening of principle 21 as a
binding precept of international law and, as such, a bolstering of what
Canada referred to at Stockholm (Chapter 5, above) as, "the secondary
consequential principle 22" and the "tertiary consequential principle
. . . (former principle 20 not now contained in the draft) on the duty
of states to inform one another considering the environmental impact
of their actions upon areas beyond their jurisdiction . . ." .

Viewed from the only reasonable perspective — from the point of
view of progress in international law-making — the Stockholm conference's achievements in the area of marine pollution were unquestionably impressive. But with French oceanographer Jacques-Yves Cousteau
reporting that from a third to half of the world's marine biota had been
killed off by man's mismanagement of the oceans over the past 20 years,
it was still necessary to ask whether it had not been another case of too
little too late. For one thing, by far the greatest quantity of toxic refuse
entering the sea was coming not from ocean dumping but from rivers
carrying the wastes of industry and agriculture. The conference endorsed literally hundreds of proposals for limiting national pollution,
but the question of whether they would be implemented was left mainly
to each nation's conscience.[3] A sobering glimpse of the enormity of the
problem the Stockholm conference had tackled was provided by the
speech in the distinguished lecture series by Norwegian anthropologist
and explorer Thor Heyerdahl:

> To visualize the immense quantities of solid and dissolved waste
> and fluid chemicals of all kinds which every minute flow into the
> ocean from the shores of all continents, we should imagine the
> ocean without water, as a big, empty depression. The fact that
> every river in the world empties into the sea without causing an
> overflow makes us subconsciously think of the ocean as a witches'
> cauldron whose contents never come out over the brim no matter
> how much is poured in. We are apt to forget that the ocean has its
> own sort of outlet: the evaporation from its surface which permits
> only pure water to escape while all our poisons, all our solid and
> dissolved wastes, are left to accumulate forever in the pot. Visualize,
> then, the ocean as a dry and empty valley ready to receive only

what Man is pouring in. The rising level of toxic matter would clearly be visible from all sides. A few examples picked at random will illustrate the input we would witness.

French rivers carry 18 billion cubic metres of liquid pollution annually into the sea; the city of Paris alone discharges almost 1.2 million cubic metres of untreated effluent into the Seine every day.

The volume of liquid waste in the Federal Republic of Germany is estimated at over nine billion cubic metres per year, or 25.4 million cubic metres per day, not counting cooling water which amounts to 33.6 million cubic metres per day. Into the Rhine alone, 50,000 tons of waste are discharged daily including 30,000 tons of sodium chloride from industrial plants.

A report of the U.N. Economic and Social Council states that we have already dumped an estimated one billion pounds of DDT into our environment and are adding an estimated hundred million pounds per year. Most of this ultimately finds its way to the ocean, blown away by wind or washed down by rain. The total world production of pesticides is estimated at over 1.3 billion pounds annually. The U.S.A. alone exports over 400 million pounds per year.

Less conspicuous than the constant flow of poisons from the shores is that even the tallest chimneys in the world send their pollutants into the ocean. The densest city smog and the darkest industrial smoke will slowly be carried away by the wind only to descend with rain and snow into the ocean. Cities and industries are expanding day by day and, so far, in America alone, waste products in the form of smoke and noxious fumes amount to a total of 390,000 tons of pollutants every day, or 142 million tons every year. The ocean is the ultimate sink for all pollution disposed of in modern communities — even what we try to send up in smoke. . . .

The whole world was upset when the *Torrey Canyon* unintentionally spilled 100,000 tons of oil in the English Channel. Every year more than 100,000 tons are intentionally pumped into the Mediterranean, an almost landlocked sea. . . . A recent study showed that for every square kilometre in the Mediterranean south of Italy there are 500 litres of solidified oil. In recent years visible pollution has begun to appear even in the largest oceans. In 1947, when the balsa raft *Kon-Tiki* crossed 4,300 miles of the Pacific, in 101 days, we on board saw no trace of man until we spotted an old wreck of a sailing ship on the coral reef where we landed. The ocean was clean and crystal clear. In 1969 it was therefore a blow to us on board the raft-ship *Ra* to observe from our papyrus bundles that entire stretches of the Atlantic Ocean were polluted. We drifted slowly past plastic containers, nylon, empty bottles and cans. Yet, most conspicuous of all was the oil. First off the African coast, next in mid ocean, and finally in front of the Caribbean islands, we drifted for days on end through water reminding us more of a city harbour than of the open sea. The surface, as far as we could see through the waves, was littered with small clots of solidified black oil, ranging in size from that of a pin head or a pea to that of a large potato. When we repeated the same general itinerary with *Ra II* the following year, in 1970, we carried out a day-by-day survey and found sporadic oil clots floating within reach of our dipnet during 43 out of the 57 days the crossing lasted. . . . In the famous Sargasso Sea, the oil lumps are now so common that recently an expedition of marine biologists had to give up working with dragnets on the surface, since the mesh of their nets was constantly getting plugged up by solidified oil and their catches literally brought in more oil clots than seaweed . . .

Heyerdahl continued: "In spite of all this, it is not the floating oil clots we should fear the most. . . . The oil clots in the sea tell a similar story to that of the refuse on the beach. Visible pollution is seen by some as a symptom of welfare. If we want to bless its presence, however, it should be as an eye-opener. . . . It is the lost contents and not the empty containers that should worry us. Where is the spray, the paste, the powder, the liquid no longer inside the empty packing . . . ?"

*   *   *

In November 1972, delegates from 78 nations and observers from 13 others met at London, in accordance with the Stockholm agreement, to put the finishing touches on the pact to limit ocean dumping. The meeting, called the International Conference on the Convention on the Dumping of Wastes at Sea, had been planned to last a week, but was extended by three days while compromise was hammered out on some of the more contentious clauses. The agreement which emerged was opened for signature on December 29, two days before the deadline imposed at Stockholm.

Unlike the Stockholm conference, the London gathering was attended by the Soviet Union with its Warsaw Pact allies, and thus provided observers with a first indication of how the Stockholm accords were likely to fare at the hands of the eastern powers. Relief was considerable when the Soviet Union, while refusing to allow any specific mention of the Stockholm conference in the ocean dumping agreement, permitted verbatim inclusion of principle 21 of the Declaration on the Human Environment in the preamble to the agreement. The U.S.S.R. thus joined the nations of Stockholm in acknowledging the principle of state responsibility for extraterritorial environmental damage. It was finally clear that the eastern nations were going to make no attempt to scuttle the Stockholm agreements.

The ocean dumping agreement also provided legal recognition, for the first time, of the right of coastal states to exercise anti-pollution authority over ships sailing in waters adjacent to their shores, simply by noting (in article 13) the need for further definition of the nature and extent of that right. Until future law of the sea conferences had resolved the issue, it was expected that most states would limit the exercise of their authority to enforce the convention to areas in which they already exercised authority over fisheries.

Virtually no significant changes in technical aspects of the agreement, as it had emerged from Ottawa and Reykjavik, were made: the black and grey lists remained, as did provisions for consultation. However, two articles of significance were added at London; one of them was made public and the other amounted to a secret accord. The public article was an escape clause insisted on by the American delegation, and it represented a substantial weakening of the accord. It had been mainly responsible for the disagreement which forced the conference into its three overtime days. Article 5 of the agreement reads:

> The provisions of article 4 [outlining the black list and grey list and the limits imposed on dumping materials referred to in these lists] shall not apply when it is necessary to secure the safety of human life or of vessels, aircraft, platforms or other man-made structures at sea in cases of *force majeure* caused by stress of weather, or in any case which constitutes a danger to human life or a real threat to vessels, aircraft, platforms or other man-made structures at sea, if dumping appears to be the only way of averting the threat and if there is every probability that the damage consequent upon such dumping will be less than would otherwise occur. Such dumping shall be so conducted as to minimize the likelihood of damage to human or marine life and shall be reported forthwith to the organization [the body responsible for administering the agreement].
>
> A contracting party may issue a special permit as an exception to article 4(1a) [the black list] in emergencies posing unacceptable risks relating to human health and admitting no other feasible solution. Before doing so, the party shall consult any other country or countries that are likely to be affected and the organization which, after consulting other parties and international organizations as appropriate shall ... promptly recommend to the party the most appropriate procedures to adopt. The party shall follow these recommendations to the maximum extent feasible and consistent with the time within which action must be taken and with the general obligation to avoid damage to the marine environment and shall inform the organization of the action it takes. The parties pledge to assist one another in such situations.
>
> Any contracting party may waive its rights under [the above paragraph] at the time of, or subsequent to, ratification of or accession to this convention.

The nations objecting to inclusion of this article in the accord (led by Canada, Spain, Portugal, India and Mexico) did so because the concept of extenuating circumstances was already well established in international law, as it is in the domestic law of most nations, and there seemed therefore no reason to include an emergency clause. On the other hand, they argued, the mere fact of its existence would virtually guarantee that it would be used — as a loophole in a tax system guarantees avoidance of tax. But the Americans were adamant, and the article quoted was as far as they could be pushed by way of a compromise. By including the waiver provision in the final paragraph the smaller nations hoped it might be possible to isolate those countries subscribing to the escape clause: the provisions for consultation and notification, it was hoped, would provide some further guarantee against its wholesale exploitation.

The second, and secret, addition to the convention made at London was less complicated: it simply exempted Japan, the world's worst industrial polluter, from the treaty's prohibition on dumping of mercury, a black-list substance, for a period of five years. Because this arrangement was not mentioned in the official conference documentation, and because it was agreed to in secret, it has been impossible to learn any more about it than the fact of its existence. One can only wonder how the representatives of the nations attending the conference justified keeping this potentially vital piece of information from the citizens back home.

NOTES

1. All the following place restrictions on the conduct of potential polluters of the oceans: the 1958 Geneva Convention on the High Seas; the 1958 Geneva Convention on the Continental Shelf; the 1954 International Convention for the Prevention of Pollution of the Sea by Oil (amended in 1962 and 1969); the 1957 International Convention Relating to the Limitation of the Liability of Owners of Seagoing Ships; the 1962 Convention on the Liability of Operators of Nuclear Ships; the 1963 Treaty Banning Nuclear Weapons Tests in the Atmosphere, in Outer Space and Under Water; the 1969 International Convention Relating to Intervention on the High Seas in Cases of Oil Pollution Casualties (not yet in force); the 1971 International Convention on the Establishment of an International Fund for Compensation for Oil Pollution Damage (not yet in force); the 1972 Oslo Convention for the Prevention of Marine Pollution by Dumping from Ships and Aircraft (which applies only to the region of the North Sea and North Atlantic).

2. The U.S. vote favouring referral of the dumping convention was subject to the following qualification, as stated in the U.S. end-of-conference report: "The U.S. does not accept that (anything in the document) constitutes endorsement of jurisdiction other than that widely accepted in international law. It believes appropriate controls on nuclear-defence vessels should be national controls taking into account recommendations of the International Atomic Energy Agency and other competent agencies, which governments should undertake to follow as closely as possible."

3. Delegations were not, in fact, expected to consider in detail the recommendations for national action (as distinct from international action), but to "refer them to the attention of governments for such action as they deem appropriate".

U.S. Rebukes Sweden Over Ecocide Issue

STOCKHOLM — *In the first harsh international exchange of the U.N. environmental conference, the U.S. tonight roundly rebuked Sweden for injecting a denunciation of "ecocide" into the conference proceedings.*

Referring to a statement by Sweden's Premier Olaf Palme at the conference's main session yesterday, Russell E. Train, chairman of the U.S. delegation said, "The United States strongly objects to what it considers a gratuitous politicizing of our environmental discussions."

"Ecocide" is broadly defined as environmentally destructive acts.

"The U.S. has continuously urged and sought full discussion and resolution of these issues in the proper fora," Mr. Train said. "This conference is not the proper place. I am personally an environmentalist and not a politician. I wish to see the U.N. conference on the human environment a success. I wish to see us work together in a spirit of positive co-operation for development and for global environmental protection. The injection of a highly charged issue by the prime minister can only do a disservice to this objective. The U.S. takes strong exception to these remarks, as Sweden is serving as the host government," he said in a formal statement.

Premier Palme, in Sweden's opening position statement on the conference's second day yesterday, enumerated various points in the 114-nation assembly's proposed declaration of environmental principles.

"It is terrifying," he said, "that to quote the draft declaration, 'immense resources continue to be consumed in armaments and armed conflict, wasting and threatening still further the human environment.' It is shocking that only preliminary discussions of this matter have been possible so far in the U.N. and at the conferences of the International Red Cross, where it has been taken up by my country and others. We fear that the active use of these methods is coupled by a passive resistance to discuss them."

The New York *Times,* June 8, 1972

Chapter seven

The outer conferences

Early in the process of planning for the Stockholm conference, the U.N. preparatory committee recognized the fact that it was concerned individuals and non-governmental organizations — not politicians — who had brought the environmental crisis to the world's attention. The committee made provision for an Environment Forum to run concurrently with the official conference, where these individuals and organizations would be able to air their views in the assembled presence of the world press. It was to be a kind of official conscience for the U.N. conference delegates. At the same time, a number of other alternative conferences were being planned to play a comparable role. They included a gathering of about thirty scientists from around the world sponsored by an organization called Dai Dong — an outgrowth of the older International Fellowship of Reconciliation. (The name "Dai Dong" comes from a pre-Confucian Chinese concept of a world in which "not only a man's family is his family, not only his children are his children, but all the world is his family and all the children are his.") Amply funded by a bequest from the inventor of the Xerox copier, the organization set itself two principal goals: drafting an alternative declaration on the human environment which, they said, was bound to be superior to the U.N. document because its drafters would not be subject to vested political interests, and convening a two-day convention on "ecocidal war" in south-east Asia.

A third parallel conference, *Folkets Forum* ("People's Forum") was organized by a coalition of a number of Scandinavian political and environmental groups. In literature published before the U.N. conference had even begun, the forum declared that "the actions of the U.N. conference on the human environment will not be based on any fundamental analysis of the problems. Many central issues will be ignored because they are controversial. The conference decisions will not be of decisive importance in stopping environmental destruction." The forum set as its task an examination of various environmental questions within the framework of a series of five questions that were, given the organizers' avowedly Marxist leanings, largely rhetorical: "Who are the victims of environmental destruction? Who benefits from environmental destruction? What is the role of the profit motive in the

origins of environmental destruction? What are the connections between environmental problems and social and cultural factors? What
changes are necessary in order to solve environmental problems? Can or
cannot these changes be made within the framework of the present
society?" POWWOW, the Swedish steering committee which had conceived and organized the forum conference, spent its time conducting
demonstrations during the conference and distributing a pamphlet
entitled, "Don't trust the U.N. Conference." It accused conference
planners of ignoring such questions as limits to economic growth, the
population explosion, and the uneven distribution of resources.

At an abandoned airport called Skarpnäck on Stockholm's outskirts,
a group of young and not-so-young Americans of the counter culture set
up yet another centre of activity. It included the sixty-odd men and
women and three Day-Glo-painted buses of Hog Farm, a kind of digger
organization which saw its job as providing food and drink and otherwise "keeping things cool" at counter-culture festivals. Perhaps best
known for their role in helping to feed the half-million youths who
attended the epochal Woodstock festival, they had been flown to Stockholm by Life Forum, an organization created by Stuart Brand. Brand is
one of the heroic figures of the American counter culture, formerly one
of Ken Kesey's Merry Pranksters, the group immortalized in Tom
Wolfe's *The Electric Kool-Aid Acid Test*. He had lately become a
millionaire with the success of his *Whole Earth Catalogue*. The $75,000
budget for the Skarpnäck village, which included a large tent farm and
a sound stage for rock musicians, had been put together by Brand partly
with the royalties from the *Whole Earth Catalogue* and partly with a
grant from the Kaplan Foundation — identified by the New York *Times*
in days gone by as one of the organizations through which the American
Central Intelligence Agency funded its projects. This fact was not to
go unnoticed.

Brand's group also included members of an American Indian organization called the Black Mesa, which had been organized to protest strip
mining for coal on Black Mesa mountain in the American south west.
The mountain is important to the Hopi Indian religion in which it is
regarded as the spiritual centre of North America. Others who travelled
to Stockholm under Life Forum's auspices were the American poets
Michael McClure and Gary Snyder and *Clear Creek* magazine's Mary
Jean Haley, who published a useful free-distribution digger guide to
Stockholm and calendar of conference-time events. And one should not
forget Wavy Gravy, Hog Farm's most famous member, who had by now
discarded his meat suit ("It was mostly salami — the ham wouldn't stay

in one piece") for a more sedate jester's cap and patch-work romper suit set off by a long staff with feathers in the end. Among all the Americans in Stockholm for the conference, only Shirley Temple Black, who was described by Michael Davie in *The Observer* as "a friendly lady with the slightly dazed social manner of someone constantly meeting people who know her name but whom she doesn't know," was to receive more coverage in the European press.

Given the "turn on, tune in, drop out" philosophy of the one and the intensely serious political activism of the other, it was probably inevitable that friction should develop between Life Forum and *Folkets Forum*. Brand had arrived in Stockholm in March, with a representative of the Kaplan Foundation, to offer *Folkets Forum* $40,000 for the right to share the Scandinavian group's elaborate conference facilities and receive its sanction for Life Forum's plans to set up a tent city for the 100,000 to 400,000 youths Brand was expecting to descend on Stockholm from all corners of the globe. After a series of progressively more angry meetings, *Folkets Forum* decided it would have nothing to do with what it saw as a highly-suspicious collection of American degenerates, dope addicts and ne'er-do-wells.

Brand next tried the Environment Forum. He described the ensuing conversation this way: "Initially I, Melissa Savage [of the *Whole Earth Catalogue*] and David Padua [of the Kaplan Foundation] came here around April. We are saying around to people, 'Are you ready for the crowds of young people?' "

" 'But they did not say it, you said it?'

" 'Right, it may happen, are you guys ready for it?'

" 'For what?'

" 'For the crowds of young people.'

" 'Why would they come?'

" 'Because everyone is interested in saving the world, especially young people.'

" 'But they mustn't come, you must tell them not to come,' they said to us, as if we could push a button somewhere and kids wouldn't come. So we said that we can't control that, but we can help you handle it if it happens, because, if it happens and it's not handled well, Stockholm would be a shambles and the U.N. conference would be a shambles and that would be a shame. But there are things we can do that might prevent that and might make it feel instead even better than if the kids never came. Because if they come and it works and it feels good and the U.N. gets some of that good feeling and there is a free stage which feels good, then the whole of Stockholm starts to cook."

However, the Environment Forum organization was in such a state of chaos at that time that it was in no position to either accept or dismiss Brand's overtures. In the end, Life Forum was to receive permission to establish itself in Stockholm from the city council and the police department, both of which tended to grow rigid at the thought of another Woodstock developing in the city at the same time that they would have their hands full with the U.N. conference. They were ready to accept all the help they could get. Life Forum was given the Skarpnäck site, which was a safe hour-long subway and train ride from the city centre where the official conference activities were to take place. As it turned out, only a few hundred young people came to Stockholm for the conference, anyway.

In its way, the Skarpnäck village symbolized the dominant American approach to the environmental crisis in all its apolitical, naively romantic, transcendental glory. While European youths concerned themselves with the gloomy political questions that lay behind the economic disparities between rich and poor nations, with colonialism and economic imperialism and with capitalism-versus-socialism, trying to clarify the relations of all these issues to the threat to the environment, the young Americans involved themselves more with symptomology, with resource depletion and wildlife conservation. It was interesting, if discouraging, to observe how the official American delegation to the U.N. conference adopted this "politics no, environment yes" attitude represented by Brand and his followers, as a means of avoiding or obscuring potentially embarrassing political issues which, for a major imperialist nation like the United States, were legion.

It was difficult to avoid concluding that this was why the American delegation allied itself with the Skarpnäck group to make a major issue out of a recommendation in subject area 2 (environmental aspects of natural resources management) that nations consider an international agreement calling for a ten-year moratorium of whaling. A save-the-whales rally held at Skarpnäck was addressed by Walter Hickel, the genial former U.S. secretary of the interior, and while the Skarpnäck group was throwing its theatrical talent behind a huge anti-whaling parade the following day, the American delegation presented impassioned speeches in support of the moratorium inside the U.N. committee. An amendment proposed by the U.S. delegation significantly strengthened the original recommendation, calling as it did for an immediate request to the International Whaling Commission (I.W.C.) to implement the moratorium "as a matter of urgency". (The I.W.C., composed of the world's major whaling nations, meets regularly behind closed doors to set international quotas on catches.) While it was clear to all delegates that several species of whales were in serious danger of extinction, it was just as obvious that the I.W.C., the only body capable of controlling the harvest, would no more consider an immediate moratorium on killing of all species than General Motors would consider a moratorium on automobile production. Hence the delicate phrasing of the original recommendation from the preparatory committee, which had simply urged a strengthening of the I.W.C. and left it to all nations to consider drafting an agreement calling for a moratorium.

In the emotion-charged atmosphere surrounding the committee debate, a suggestion by Japan, that the moratorium be applied only to species considered endangered or depleted, was rejected, as were other compromises that would have left the I.W.C. with some room to manoeuvre. The result was predictable: although the American amendment sailed through to cheers from the public gallery by a vote of 51 for, three opposed (Japan, Portugal and South Africa) and 12 abstentions, the I.W.C., meeting in London just 20 days later, rejected the call for a moratorium by a vote of 4-6-4. Of the 51 nations voting in favour of the moratorium during the highly-publicized Stockholm debate, eight were members of the I.W.C.: the U.S., Britain, Mexico, Argentina, France, Denmark, Norway and Canada. However, in the privacy of the I.W.C. meeting, only the first four again voted in favour of the moratorium proposal. Canada, Denmark and France chose to abstain this time and Norway voted "no".[1] Iceland and Panama, who had abstained in Stockholm, also switched their votes to "no" in London. (The results of the I.W.C. vote were made public by U.S. delegate Russell Train after his motion to open the meeting to the press failed to find a seconder, and was not even debated.) It is scarcely necessary to point out that the actions of the I.W.C., predictable though they had been, did nothing to enhance the prestige of the Stockholm conference.

Dai Dong's sponsorship of the "convention on ecocidal war" produced a considerable success in exposing the extreme destruction done to the Indochinese environment by United States forces in bombing, defoliation, and forest-removal operations. The other activities of the group were, however, little more helpful than those of Life Forum. It was one of the more notable ironies of the conference that this group of supposedly objective, politically-unattached academics had less success in drafting its alternative declaration on the human environment than the U.N. conference had with the official document. The scientists, representing all areas of the globe except the Soviet bloc countries, met for two weeks, beginning the week before the U.N. conference opened.

At the end of that time, the draft document which had been prepared in advance (in the same way as the U.N. conference delegates were to discuss a prepared draft) emerged much weakened by a series of compromises dictated mainly by political rather than scientific considerations.

Dai Dong's most notable failure to reach agreement came in the area of population control, a subject which all the alternative conferences accused the U.N. gathering of deliberately ignoring as overly controversial. This was not entirely accurate: while the U.N. conference was not asked to treat the question in any depth, there was an implicit understanding throughout the preparatory committee documents that population growth was a key factor in the environmental crisis as well as in the difficulties experienced by many developing nations in trying to raise living standards. Moreover, the U.N. had already planned a full-dress conference on population for 1974. Strong and other officials argued that it was unnecessary to deal with the subject in detail at Stockholm.

There were at least two specific recommendations concerning population control in the U.N. documents. A recommendation in the Human Settlements paper stated that "the World Health Organization and other U.N. agencies should increase assistance in the field of family planning programmes without delay," and that "W.H.O. should promote and intensify research endeavours in the field of human reproduction, so that serious consequences of the population explosion on the human environment can be prevented." This provoked a long debate which revealed deep differences of opinion on the subject among non-industrialized nations. The delegate from the Holy See (the Vatican) spoke for several Latin American nations when he said: "It is by no means proved that an excess in population leads to a decline in environmental quality." At the same time a majority of the developing nations expressed support for population-control measures. A spokesman for the Indian delegation described his nation's energetic efforts in the cause of family planning and declared that they were paying dividends; the delegate from Uganda, where the current birth rate of 3.8 per cent was expected to rise by 1985 to 4.6 per cent (doubling time: 16 years), called the recommendation "one of the most important recommendations that could come out of this conference". The vote following the debate was 55 for, 18 against.

The Declaration on the Human Environment also dealt specifically with population: the document's preamble stated that "the natural growth of population continuously presents problems on the preservation of the environment, and adequate policies and measures should be adopted, as appropriate, to face these problems." Principle 16 of the document elaborated: "Demographic policies, which are without prejudice to basic human rights and which are deemed appropriate by the governments concerned, should be applied in those regions where the rate of population growth or excessive population concentrations are likely to have adverse effects on the environment or development, or where low population density may prevent improvement of the human environment and impede development."

In view of the frightening statistical evidence of the really crushing overpopulation problem looming just over the horizon, it was arguable that these references scarcely added up to a forceful statement. On the other hand, it was difficult to deny the logic of the U.N. position that such a contentious problem was best dealt with, as planned, at a separate conference where delegates would be able to give it their undivided attention. In any case, Dai Dong's own comments on the matter were even less to the point. The relevant paragraphs of the scientists' declaration ran:

> It is obvious that human population growth cannot continue indefinitely in a finite environment with finite resources. At the same time, population is one of a number of factors, none of which in the long run is the most important or the most decisive in affecting the human environment. In fact, the question of population is intrinsically inseparable from the question of access to resources. A true improvement in the living conditions of the people of developing countries would go further in stabilizing population growth than programs of population control. Thus, population is not a single global or biological problem, but one which has a complex interrelationship with the social, economic and natural environments of man. Population size may be too small or too large at any particular time depending on the availability of natural resources and the stresses on the environment. The ecological principle regarding the role of population is equally applicable to human and animal populations. However, in human populations social organization is such that massive maldistribution of essential resources is practised.
>
> On a global scale, the population problems of the developing countries have coincided with the colonial expansions of the last two centuries, and the virtual exclusion of the populations of Asia, Africa and Latin America from full access to their own resources. This process of economic exploitation still continues in spite of the nominal independence of various former colonies and dependencies. Meanwhile political control by economic elites in the developing countries make it impossible for the people of the third world to use the resources to cater to their own needs. The redistribution of resources on a global level is an unconditional prerequisite for correcting this historic process.

As long as resources are wasted, as they manifestly are, it is deceptive to describe population growth as if this were the source of all evils. (There is obviously a confusion in many peoples' minds between overcrowding and population.) The fact that some urban areas grow like cancers should not serve as a pretext to divert attention from the real task of our generation, which is to achieve proper management of resources and space. Those nations that are mainly responsible for this state of affairs have certainly no right to recommend population-stabilizing policies to the world's hungry peoples.

It should be noted that, for economically developed countries, the combination of an increase in consumption per capita with a stable population, or of a stable consumption per capita with a growing population, will both lead to further resource depletion and pollution. This would not be true if the appropriate socio-economic changes that will lead to ecologically sound production and consumption patterns are made.

That this statement contained so much narrow, facile political dogma was unfortunate; that those small portions of it presented as scientific fact were so open to serious question was unforgivable. Six of the Dai Dong scientists were to express their embarrassment with this section of the declaration by agreeing to sign the document only after the following statement of interpretation had been added:[2]

In several parts of this document, the environmental issues have become largely submerged in statements more relevant in one of a number of ideological polarities. A current controversy, concerning the quantitative measure of significance to be attached at this point in time to the various aspects of "population factor" in comparison to other important factors, has confused the issue. The differences provoking the scientific controversy in themselves do not concern directly the point we make here; in various places and at various times the "population issue" has become or will become critical, being preceded or followed in time by other critical factors not closely related to the population factor.

The Dai Dong declaration did little better on any of the other environmental issues it tackled: everywhere, cool logic was swamped by political rhetoric. In its attempt to be as "democratic" as possible (in contrast to the U.N. conference, which, it was assumed, would be dominated by the rich and powerful nations) Dai Dong did not structure its debates around any formal rules of procedure. As a result it left itself open to the possibility of being dominated by almost any determined group or individual with an axe to grind. This was exactly what had happened: the political views expressed throughout the Dai Dong declaration were largely those of a young, self-proclaimed spokesman for third-world interests named M. Taghi Farvar. Farvar, an Iranian who had spent much of his mature life in the U.S., was a protégé of the American environmentalist Barry Commoner and a graduate student in Commoner's Centre for the Biology of Natural Systems in Washington University, St. Louis.

Farvar and Commoner would team up to effectively dominate the U.N.-sanctioned Environmental Forum as well. From its inception in the U.N. preparatory committee in 1971 the Environment Forum had been plagued by a shortage of funds. By the time budgetary problems were solved in January, 1972, by a grant of $86,000 from the Swedish government, there was little time left to organize a coherent programme out of the 220 suggestions submitted by non-governmental organizations around the world. Dissension among the staff wasted most of what little time did remain, with the result that when Commoner arrived — invited as a founder of the U.S.-based Scientists' Institute for Public Information (S.I.P.I.) — there was a leadership vacuum waiting to be filled. And fill it he did, with the assistance of Farvar and the Iranian's own "O.I." Group of scientists and students (from *Ote Iwapo* — "count everything"), united in the opinion that population counted for little in the equation of environmental deterioration. Commoner shared this view, although he had arrived at the conclusion by a different line of reasoning. While Farvar and the O.I. Group were for the most part reacting to their visceral feeling that family planning was a racist plot designed to keep the northern, white nations on top of the heap, Commoner did his best to define the politically loaded overpopulation question out of existence, arguing instead that environmental degradation was almost entirely the result of widespread use of "faulty" technology in the industrialized nations — "faulty", because it placed economic considerations above ecological ones. Commoner's viewpoint had recently been elaborated in his book *The Closing Circle*, and had stirred acrimonious controversy among American environmentalists, some of whom felt Commoner was encouraging a public apathy about population growth that was potentially disastrous. The debate had recently surfaced in the April, 1972 issue of *Environment* magazine, in which *The Closing Circle* had been the subject of a brutal review by Paul Ehrlich (author of *The Population Bomb*) and his colleague John P. Holdren, with an equally virulent rebuttal from Commoner.

The result of the Commoner-Farvar takeover of the Environment Forum was described with typical irreverence in the Stockholm conference *Eco*:

> On Friday, when International Planned Parenthood Federation and World Wildlife Fund representatives tried to stage a debate on

the relationship of population growth to natural resource depletion, the [forum] organizers flatly refused to give Paul Ehrlich any
chance to develop his case. Indeed, right in the midst of a press
conference, the O.I. boys (and girls) moved in a posse on to the
platform and took over the meeting, adding four of their number
to the three panelists, who were already two-to-one against the view
that population and the environment should be related.

The scene was all set for the destruction of Ehrlich. Commoner,
masterminding the debunking, had refused to meet Ehrlich in a
direct confrontation. Instead, he lurked in the gallery (of the
auditorium), ventriloquizing to his puppet army by means of
scribbled instructions carried downstairs, while Farvar, the chief
lieutenant, wandered round the forum prompting and orchestrat-
ing his O.I. boys. At one point an incensed Ehrlich called out,
"Where's Barry baby?" and challenged Commoner to face him in
debate there and then. But "Barry baby" would not budge. He
obviously preferred the spectacle of Ehrlich facing a 2-1 panel and
a hostile audience.

The confrontation had its positive aspect, however. The atmosphere of elitist conspiracy was so prevalent that it provoked liberal
family-planning advocates in the audience to ask what right the
all-male panel had to speak for the women of Africa and Latin
America and to assume that they would not want to limit their
families if they could. Ehrlich, unable to present his case or argue
it properly, nevertheless managed to put over the message that he
counted everything rather more thoroughly than the O.I. boys, and
that his proposal of rich nation de-development and of poor nation
semi-development was, in redistributive terms, at least as radical as
that of his doctrinaire opponents. He did not, however, have the
naivety to believe that redistribution alone would solve everything,
(arguing) that a shift away from material values and toward new
political avenues must be pragmatically sought as well.

This sort of pragmatism over political systems was too much for
Farvar, however. When, during a [later] panel debate, he was asked
why the forum organizers refused to allow two-sided debates on
some environmental issues . . . he said that the trouble was that the
other side "could not be objective".

One trouble with the rule of the forum by pseudo-leftist elitists
who claim to speak for the third world (although they mostly live
on American campuses and in some cases have not been back home
to their own countries for years) is that they are so boring: insisting
on endless monologues (even from the meeting chairmen) which
have simply driven forum visitors away. But the more serious
trouble is that there is very little discussion of the environmental
issues themselves and of what can be done about them by willing
and energetic individuals and non-government organizations . . .

The Environment Forum's own daily conference news-sheet printed
a reply which, despite its brevity, spoke volumes:

On Wednesday, the Stockholm conference *Eco* was so hard up for ideas about serious environment problems that it devoted a whole page to a snide and bitchy history of how the Environment Forum was taken over by "semi-Marxists" (a word of abuse in the anonymous writer's vocabulary), plus some vicious personal attacks on those running it. Coming from the *Eco*, which reads like neo-Fascist anti-third-world literature one day, and liberal "semi-Marxist" journalism the next, according to who, from its environment-is-more-important-than-politics team, is editing it, this was perhaps all one could expect. They would have done better to take the trouble to cover the forum's panels on the dangers of cancer caused by irresponsible capitalism . . .

Only the *Folkets Forum*, with its openly and unambiguously left-wing political bias, was able to avoid the mire of opportunism and recrimination which had been the nemesis of the other "conscience" conferences. But even this group managed to strain its credibility seriously before the conference had ended. At a press conference held as the U.N. gathering was winding up its business, *Folkets Forum* organizers presented evidence which they said showed that not only Life Forum, but also S.I.P.I. (Commoner's group) had received funding from the notorious Kaplan Foundation. The organizers concluded from this that the C.I.A. had tried to manipulate the course of events at Stockholm by taking the spotlight away from those (like themselves) who had been arguing that an improved human environment demanded an end to capitalism. Whether or not the charge was true (and who was there remaining so foolhardy as to dismiss the possibility of the C.I.A.'s involvement in anything?), it had just the right tone to provide a fitting conclusion to the activities of the alternative conferences. If these meetings had achieved little else, they had served to highlight the successes of the U.N. conference, making them seem, by contrast, all the more remarkable.

NOTES

1. On December 22, 1972, the Canadian government announced unilaterally that it was imposing an immediate ban on commercial whaling of all large species within the country's east-coast fishing jurisdiction. Whaling off Canada's west coast had come to an end in 1968.
2. They were Nicholas Gorgescu-Roegen, Professor of Economics, Vanderbilt University, Nashville, Tenn.; P. J. Deoras, Medical Biologist, Haffkine Institute, Bombay; Bengt Hubendick, Head, Museum of Natural History, Goteborg, Sweden; Donald A. Chant, Chairman of the Zoology Department, University of Toronto; Henry Regier, Professor of Zoology, University of Toronto; Fred Knelman, Professor, Humanities and Science Department, Sir George Williams University, Montreal.

Nairobi Gets U.N. Office to Monitor Pollution

UNITED NATIONS (CP) — *The General Assembly's economics committee ignored Western objections yesterday, and voted overwhelmingly to establish the U.N.'s environmental secretariat in Nairobi.*

The vote of 93 to 1 with 30 abstentions came after a strong appeal from developing and non-aligned countries to have a U.N. headquarters located outside New York and western Europe.

The United States cast the lone negative vote and Canada was among the 30 members who abstained...

A U.N. estimate prepared before the vote said it would cost $2.4 million to establish and operate the environment secretariat in Nairobi, the highest cost of any centre considered.

Geneva would have been the least costly of other possibilities at $1.3 million while the New York cost was set at $1.5 million.

The developing countries argued that the U.N. has a global constituency and should be willing to reach out to it. The debate was marked by increasing rancor at points as representatives of developing countries accused the more wealthy members of ignoring their concerns.

The Daily Star (Toronto), November 11, 1972

...And how are we going to know if the conference has been a success? One simple test will be whether Strong emerges at the head of a continuing U.N. environmental organization, since he will not take such a job unless he thinks it has teeth. Strong looks utterly insignificant — like one of the balloon men you can buy in America and put on the seat of your car to fool attackers. But he has astounding energy and resourcefulness. If he takes a new U.N. job, you can take evens about the biosphere surviving. If he doesn't — stock up on whole wheat.

Michael Davie in *The Observer* (London), June 11, 1972

Epilogue

Late in December of 1972, the 27th U.N. General Assembly, meeting in New York, gave final approval to the decisions taken at the Stockholm conference. A new environment secretariat was set up, financed through a voluntary fund with an initial $100 million over five years, and Maurice Strong selected to head the new agency which was to be headquartered in Nairobi, Kenya. The action plan worked out in Stockholm was accepted virtually without change (Appendix 3). As expected, the U.S.S.R. and its allies abstained — and thus acquiesced — throughout the voting. It seemed likely that future historians would see these actions as some of the most significant ever taken by the world body. If the U.N. had had little success in achieving greater world co-operation through the classical means of moral suasion, perhaps more would be accomplished under the relentless pressure of global pollution and the necessity of working together to protect the natural environment. In the environmental secretariat, the U.N. had found a new and compellingly understandable *raison d'être*, a new and impregnable defence against those who would argue that the 27-year-old organization had proven itself useless and irrelevant and therefore expendable. The fight to preserve the global environment required international action, and only the U.N. was equipped to encourage and co-ordinate that action.

There was one major disappointment: principle 20 of the draft Declaration on the Human Environment, referred to the General Assembly at Brazil's insistence, was not re-inserted into the declaration. Once again Brazil was able to capitalize on the big powers' lukewarm support for the idea of states' responsibility to consult with their neighbours before undertaking projects with possible trans-boundary environmental effects, to push through a resolution that was laughably innocuous when compared with the original principle. The operative paragraphs of the Brazil-sponsored resolution accepted by the General Assembly read:

> [States] recognize that co-operation between states in the field of the environment, including co-operation towards the implementation of principles 21 and 22 of the Declaration of the United Nations Conference on the Human Environment, will be effectively

achieved if official public knowledge is provided of the technical data relating to the work to be carried out by states within their national jurisdiction with a view to avoiding significant harm that may occur in the human environment of the adjacent area;

[States] recognize further that the technical data referred to in the preceding paragraph will be given and received in the best spirit of co-operation and good neighbourliness, without this being construed as enabling each state to delay or impede the programmes and projects of exploration, exploitation and development of the natural resources of the states in whose territories such programmes and projects are carried out.

The word "consult", it was duly noted, appeared nowhere in the resolution. Principle 20 had been effectively erased. Those nations which had fought for the principle through the Stockholm conference and again in New York were forced to be satisfied with a resolution sponsored by Canada, Mexico, Australia, New Zealand and Panama which ensured that principles 21 and 22 of the Declaration would not be affected by Brazil's nullification of the consultation principle. It read:

The General Assembly, recalling principles 21 and 22 of the Declaration . . . on the Human Environment concerning the international responsibility of states in regard to the human environment, bearing in mind that those principles lay down the basic rules governing this matter, declares that no resolution adopted at the 27th session of the General Assembly [i.e. the Brazilian resolution] can affect principles 21 and 22 of the Declaration . . . on the Human Environment.

The picture was not entirely bleak, however; observers were able to take some cheer from the fact that the legal principle of duty to consult had been entrenched in the new ocean dumping accord agreed to in London.

A NOTE REGARDING THE APPENDICES: The account of the Stockholm conference contained in the preceding pages has been very selective in its references to the recommendations contained in the action plan; as a rule, only those issues which seemed to need further explanation or which reflected on the complex political nature of the environmental crisis have been discussed in any detail. There were, however, many resolutions passed at Stockholm and adopted by the General Assembly as part of the action plan which, though straightforward and non-controversial (like those calling for establishment of a world bank of genetic resources and others concerning the need for better environmental education programmes), were nonetheless important. The reader who is interested in making his grasp of the achievements of the conference more complete will find these contained in Appendix 3 along with the resolutions discussed in the preceding text.

The Declaration on the Human Environment contained in Appendix 2 is in the form in which the document was finally presented to the General Assembly. Because of the deletion of principle 20 of the original draft and the insertion of new material, the numbering of the paragraphs does not coincide with that used in the original as prepared by the Stockholm preparatory committee. To avoid any confusion, the original paragraph numbers have been noted in brackets after the numbers used in the final draft.

The Blueprint for Survival

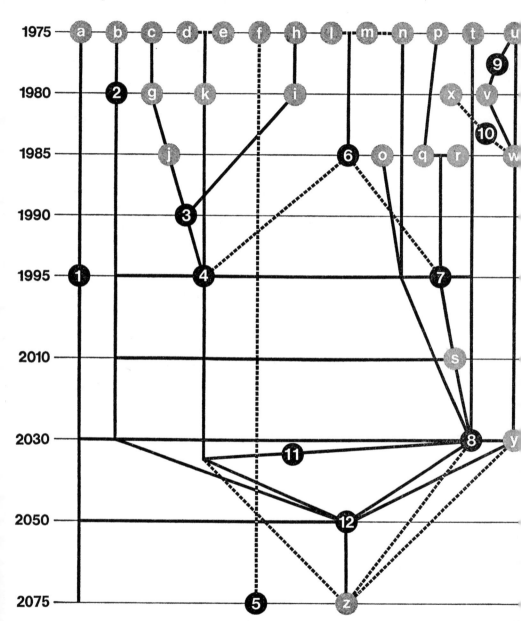

establishment of national population service

introduction of raw materials, amortisation and power taxes; antidisamenity legislation; air, land and water quality targets; recycling grants; revised social accounting systems.

) developed countries end commitment to persistent pesticides and subsidise similar move by undeveloped countries.

) end of subsidies on inorganic fertilisers.

) grants for use of organics and introduction of diversity

emergency food programme for undeveloped countries

) integrated control research programme

') integrated control training programme

) progressive substitution of nonpersistent for persistent pesticides

) progressive introduction of diversified farming practices

) substitution of integrated control for chemical control

l) end of road building

n) clearance of derelict land and beginning of renewal programme

) restrictions on private transport and subsidies for public transport

) development of rapid mass-transit

) research into materials substitution

) development of alternative technologies

) decentralisation of industry: part one (redirection)

s) decentralisation of industry: part two (development of community types)

) redistribution of government

) education research

) teacher training

w) education

x) experimental community

y) domestic sewage to land

z) target date for basic establishment of network of self-sufficient, self-regulating communities.

(1) should be operating fully by 1980; review in 1995—if replacement-size families improbable by 2000, bring in socio-economic restraints; UK population should begin to slowly decline from 2015-2020 onwards; world population from 2100; little significant feedback expected in UK until about 2030.

(2) progressive; ironing out run to eliminate inconsistencies up to 1980; thereafter revise and tighten every five years; increasingly significant feedback from 1980 onwards, stimulating materials-energy conservation, employment-intensive industry, decentralisation, and progress in direction of (p), (q), (r) and (s).

(3) limited substitution of integrated control can begin quite soon, but large-scale substitution will depend on (h) integrated control research programme; naturally (h), (i) and (j) will run in parallel and are therefore represented as one; (g) will also continue for some time.

(4) diversified farming practices. (k) and integrated control (j) will link up and form an agriculture best-suited for small, reasonably self-sufficient communities, so stimulating their development: significant feedback, therefore, will occur from this point.

(5) likely to be necessary at least until 2100.

(6) labour released from road building can go to (m) clearance of derelict land, which should be completed by 1985; thereafter there may be other renewal programmes such as canal restoration, while agriculture will increasingly require more manpower.

(7) development of alternative technologies (q) and redirecting of industry (r) will proceed in harness; progressively significant feedback between (b) and (t).

(8) target date for maximum redistribution of government 2030 to coincide with 45 years operation of (w); see note (9).

(9) five years only allowed for preliminary organisation and research, since it can proceed in harness with teacher training (v) and also with the education programme itself (w).

(10) an experimental community of 500 could be set up to clarify problems; feedback to (u).

(11) as soon as communities are small enough, domestic sewage can be returned to the land; there should be the firm beginnings of a good urban-rural mix by then.

(12) by this time there should be sufficient diversity of agriculture, decentralisation of government, together with a large proportion of people whose education is designed for life in the stable society, for the establishment of self-sufficient, self-regulating communities to be well-advanced. At this point taxation, grants, incentives, etc, could be taken over by the communities themselves. A further generation is allowed until target date, however.

Appendix II

The declaration appears here as it was adopted by the Stockholm conference. Wording added to the original draft is italicized. Where wording was altered without any addition, a note appears in brackets.

Principle 20 of the draft document, referred to the U.N. General Assembly for discussion, reads: "Relevant information must be supplied by states on activities or developments within their jurisdictions or under their control whenever they believe, or have reason to believe, that such information is needed to avoid the risk of significant adverse effects on the environment in areas beyond their national jurisdiction."

DECLARATION OF THE UNITED NATIONS CONFERENCE ON THE HUMAN ENVIRONMENT

The United Nations Conference on the Human Environment,
Having met at Stockholm from 5 to 16 June 1972,
Having considered the need for a common outlook and for common principles to inspire and guide the peoples of the world in the preservation and enhancement of the human environment,

I

Proclaims that:

1. Man is both creature and moulder of his environment, which gives him physical sustenance and affords him the opportunity for intellectual, moral, social and spiritual growth. In the long and tortuous evolution of the human race on this planet a stage has been reached when, through the rapid acceleration of science and technology, man has acquired the power to transform his environment in countless ways and on an unprecedented scale. Both aspects of man's environment, the natural and the man-made, are essential to his well-being and to the enjoyment of basic human rights — even the right to life itself.

2. *The protection and improvement of the human environment is a major issue which affects the well-being of peoples and economic development throughout the world; it is the urgent desire of the peoples of the whole world and the duty of all Governments.*

3. [Wording altered slightly.] Man has constantly to sum up experience and go on discovering, inventing, creating and advancing. In our time, man's capability to transform his surroundings, if used wisely, can bring to all peoples the benefits of development and the opportunity to enhance the quality of life. Wrongly or heedlessly applied, the same power can do incalculable harm to human beings and the

human environment. We see around us growing evidence of man-made harm in many regions of the Earth: dangerous levels of pollution in water, air, earth and living beings; major and undesirable disturbances to the ecological balance of the biosphere; destruction and depletion of irreplaceable resources; and gross deficiencies harmful to the physical, mental and social health of man, in the man-made environment, particularly in the living and working environment.

4. *In the developing countries most of the environmental problems are caused by under-development. Millions continue to live far below the minimum levels required for a decent human existence, deprived of adequate food and clothing, shelter and education, health and sanitation. Therefore, the developing countries must direct their efforts to development, bearing in mind their priorities and the need to safeguard and improve the environment. For the same purpose, the industrialized countries should make efforts to reduce the gap between themselves and the developing countries. In the industrialized countries, environmental problems are generally related to industrialization and technological development.*

5. [Wording altered.] The natural growth of population continuously presents problems on the preservation of the environment, and adequate policies and measures should be adopted, as appropriate, to face these problems. *Of all things in the world, people are the most precious. It is the people that propel social progress, create social wealth, develop science and technology and, through their hard work, continuously transform the human environment. Along with social progress and the advance of production, science and technology, the capability of man to improve the environment increases with each passing day.*

6. A point has been reached in history when we must shape our actions throughout the world with a more prudent care for their environmental consequences. Through ignorance or indifference we can do massive and irreversible harm to the earthly environment on which our life and well-being depend. Conversely, through fuller knowledge and wiser action, we can achieve for ourselves and our posterity a better life in an environment more in keeping with human needs and hopes. *There are broad vistas for the enhancement of environmental quality and the creation of a good life.* What is needed is an enthusiastic but calm state of mind and intense but orderly work. For the purpose of attaining freedom in the world of nature, man must use knowledge to build, in collaboration with nature, a better environment. To defend and improve the human environment for present and future generations has become an imperative goal for mankind — a goal to be pursued together with, and in harmony with, the established and fundamental goals of peace and of world-wide economic and social development.

7. To achieve this environmental goal will demand the acceptance of responsibility by citizens and communities and by enterprises and institutions at every level, all sharing equitably in common efforts. Individuals in all walks of life as well as organizations in many fields, by their values and the sum of their actions, will shape the world environment of the future. Local and national governments will bear the greatest burden for large-scale environmental policy and action within their jurisdictions. *International co-operation is also needed in order to raise resources to support the developing countries in carrying out their responsibilities in this field.* A growing class of environmental problems, because they are regional or global in extent or because they affect the common international realm, will require extensive co-operation among nations and action by international organizations in the common interest. *The Conference calls upon Governments and peoples to exert common efforts for the preservation and improvement of the human environment, for the benefit of all the people and for their posterity.*

II
PRINCIPLES

States the common conviction that:

Principle 1

Man has the fundamental right to freedom, equality and adequate conditions of life, in an environment of a quality that permits a life of dignity and well-being, and he bears a solemn responsibility to protect and improve the environment for present and future generations. *In this respect, policies promoting or perpetuating apartheid, racial segregation, discrimination, colonial and other forms of oppression and foreign domination stand condemned and must be eliminated.*

Principle 2

The natural resources of the earth including the air, water, land, flora and fauna and especially representative samples of natural ecosystems must be safeguarded for the benefit of present and future generations through careful planning or management, as appropriate.

Principle 3

The capacity of the earth to produce vital renewable resources must be maintained and, wherever practicable, restored or improved.

Principle 4 [new]

Man has a special responsibility to safeguard and wisely manage the heritage of wildlife and its habitat which are now gravely imperilled by a combination of adverse factors. Nature conservation including wildlife must therefore receive importance in planning for economic development.

Principle 5 [draft 4]

The non-renewable resources of the earth must be employed in such a way as to guard against the danger of their future exhaustion *and to ensure that benefits from such employment are shared by all mankind.*

Principle 6 [draft 5]

The discharge of toxic substances or of other substances *and the release of heat,* in such quantities or concentrations as to exceed the capacity of the environment to render them harmless, must be halted in order to ensure that serious or irreversible damage is not inflicted upon ecosystems. *The just struggle of the peoples of all countries against pollution should be supported.*

Principle 7 [new]

States shall take all possible steps to prevent pollution of the seas by substances that are liable to create hazards to human health, to harm living resources and marine life, to damage amenities or to interfere with other legitimate uses of the sea.

Principle 8 [draft 6]

Economic and social development is essential for ensuring a favourable living and working environment for man and for creating conditions on earth that are necessary for the improvement of the quality of life.

Principle 9 [draft 7]

Environmental deficiencies generated by the conditions of under-development and natural disasters pose grave problems and can best be remedied by accelerated development *through the transfer of substantial quantities of financial and technological assistance as a supplement to the domestic effort of the developing countries and such timely assistance as may be required.*

Principle 10 [new]

For the developing countries, stability of prices and adequate earnings for primary commodities and raw material are essential to environmental management since economic factors as well as ecological processes must be taken into account.

Principle 11 [draft 8]

The environmental policies of all States should enhance and not adversely affect the present or future development potential of developing countries, nor should they hamper the attainment of better living conditions for all, and appropriate steps should be taken by States and international organizations with a view to reaching agreement on meeting the possible national and international economic consequences resulting from the application of environmental measures.

Principle 12 [draft 9]

Resources should be made available to preserve and improve the environment, taking into account the circumstances and particular requirements of developing countries and any costs which may emanate from their incorporating environmental safeguards into their development planning and the need for making available to them, upon their request, additional international technical and financial assistance for this purpose.

Principle 13 [draft 10]

[Wording altered.] In order to achieve a more rational management of resources and thus to improve the environment, States should adopt an integrated and co-ordinated approach to their development planning so as to ensure that development is compatible with the need to protect and improve the human environment for the benefit of their population.

Principle 14 [draft 11]

Rational planning constitutes an essential tool for reconciling any conflict between the needs of development and the need to protect and improve the environment.

Principle 15 [draft 12]

Planning must be applied to human settlements and urbanization with a view to avoiding adverse effects on the environment and obtaining maximum social, economic and environmental benefits *for all. In this respect projects which are designed for colonialist and racist domination must be abandoned.*

Principle 16 [draft 13]

Demographic policies, which are without prejudice to basic human rights and which are deemed appropriate by Governments concerned, should be applied in those regions where the rate of population growth or excessive population concentrations are likely to have adverse effects on the environment or development, or where low population density may prevent improvement of the human environment and impede development.

Principle 17 [draft 14]

Appropriate national institutions must be entrusted with the task of planning, managing or controlling the environmental resources of States with the view to enhancing environmental quality.

Principle 18 [draft 15]

[Wording altered.] Science and technology, as part of their contributions to economic and social development, must be applied to the identification, avoidance and control of environmental risks and the solution of environmental problems and for the common good of mankind.

Principle 19 [draft 16]

Education in environmental matters, for the younger generation *as well as adults, giving due consideration to the underprivileged,* is essential in order to broaden the basis for an enlightened opinion and responsible conduct by individuals, enterprises and communities in protecting and improving the environment *in its full human dimension. It is also essential that mass media of communications avoid contributing to the deterioration of the environment, but, on the contrary, disseminate information of an educational nature, on the need to protect and improve the environment in order to enable man to develop in every respect.*

Principle 20 [draft 17]

[Wording altered.] Scientific research and development in the context of environmental problems, both national and multinational, must be promoted in all countries, especially the developing countries. In this connexion, the free flow of up-to-date scientific information and transfer of experience must be supported and assisted, to facilitate the solution of environmental problems; *environmental technologies should be made available to developing countries on terms which would encourage their wide dissemination without constituting an economic burden on the developing countries.*

Principle 21 [draft 18]

States have, in accordance with the Charter of the United Nations and the principles of international law, the sovereign right to exploit their own resources pursuant to their own environmental policies, and the responsibility to ensure that activities within their jurisdiction or control do not cause damage to the environment of other States or of areas beyond the limits of national jurisdiction.

Principle 22 [draft 19]

States shall co-operate to develop further the international law regarding liability and compensation for the victims of pollution and other environmental damage caused by activities within the jurisdiction or control of such States to areas beyond their jurisdiction.

Principle 23 [new]

Without prejudice to such criteria as may be agreed upon by the international community, or to standards which will have to be determined nationally, it will be essential in all cases to consider the systems of values prevailing in each country, and the extent of the applicability of standards which are valid for the most advanced countries but which may be inappropriate and of unwarranted social cost for the developing countries.

Principle 24 [draft 22]

[Wording altered.] International matters concerning the protection and improvement of the environment should be handled in a co-operative spirit by all countries, big or small, on an equal footing. Co-operation through multilateral or bilateral arrangements or other appropriate means is essential to effectively control, prevent, reduce and eliminate adverse environmental effects resulting from activities conducted in all spheres, in such a way that due account is taken of the sovereignty and interests of all States.

Principle 25 [draft 23]

States shall ensure that international organizations play a co-ordinated, efficient and dynamic role for the protection and improvement of the environment.

Principle 26 [draft 21]

Man and his environment must be spared the effects of nuclear weapons and all other means of mass destruction. *States must strive to reach prompt agreement, in the relevant international organs, on the elimination and complete destruction of such weapons.*

Appendix III

*The Stockholm Conference Action Plan as approved by the 27th
United Nations General Assembly*

ACTION PLAN FOR THE HUMAN ENVIRONMENT

A. *Framework for environmental action*

The recommendations adopted by the Conference for the substantive items on the agenda of the Conference are set out in chapter II, section B, below. The recommendations have been grouped, in section C, in an Action Plan that makes it possible to identify international programmes and activities across the boundaries of all subject areas. The broad types of action that make up the Plan are:

(*a*) The global environmental assessment programme (Earthwatch);

(*b*) Environmental management activities;

(*c*) International measures to support the national and international actions of assessment and management.

The framework of the Action Plan is illustrated in the following diagram.

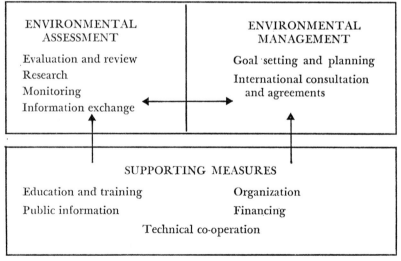

B. *Recommendations for action at the international level*

The texts of the recommendations adopted by the United Nations Conference on the Human Environment are given below.

Planning and management of human settlements
for environmental quality

Recommendation 1

The planning, improvement and management of rural and urban settlements demand an approach, at all levels, which embraces all aspects of the human environment, both natural and man-made. Accordingly, *it is recommended*:

(*a*)   That all development assistance agencies, whether international, such as the United Nations Development Programme and the International Bank for Reconstruction and Development, regional or national, should in their development assistance activities also give high priority within available resources to requests from Governments for assistance in the planning of human settlements, notably in housing, transportation, water, sewerage and public health, the mobilization of human and financial resources, the improvement of transitional urban settlements and the provision and maintenance of essential community services, in order to achieve as far as possible the social well-being of the receiving country as a whole;

(*b*)   That these agencies also be prepared to assist the less industrialized countries in solving the environmental problems of development projects; to this end they should actively support the training and encourage the recruitment of requisite personnel, as far as possible within these countries themselves.

Recommendation 2

1.   *It is recommended* that Governments should designate to the Secretary-General areas in which they have committed themselves (or are prepared to commit themselves) to a long-term programme of improvement and global promotion of the environment.

(*a*)   In this connexion, countries are invited to share internationally all relevant information on the problems they encounter and the solutions they devise in developing these areas.

(*b*)   Countries concerned will presumably appoint an appropriate body to plan such a programme, and to supervise its implementation, for areas which could vary in size from a city block to a national region; presumably, too, the programme will be designated to serve, among other purposes, as a vehicle for the preparation and launching of experimental and pilot projects.

(*c*)   Countries which are willing to launch an improvement programme should be prepared to welcome international co-operation, seeking the advice or assistance of competent international bodies.

2.   *It is further recommended*:

(*a*)   That in order to ensure the success of the programme, Governments should urge the Secretary-General to undertake a process of planning and co-ordination whereby contact would be established with nations likely to participate in the programme; international teams of experts might be assembled for that purpose;

(*b*)   That a Conference/Demonstration on Experimental Human Settlements should be held under the auspices of the United Nations in order to provide for co-ordination and the exchange of information and to demonstrate to world public opinion the potential of this approach by means of a display of experimental projects;

(*c*)   That nations should take into consideration Canada's offer to organize such a Conference/Demonstration and to act as host to it.

Recommendation 3

Certain aspects of human settlements can have international implications, for example, the "export" of pollution from urban and industrial areas, and the effects of seaports on international hinterlands. Accordingly, *it is recommended* that the attention of Governments be drawn to the need to consult bilaterally or regionally whenever environmental conditions or development plans in one country could have repercussions in one or more neighbouring countries.

Recommendation 4

1. *It is recommended* that Governments and the Secretary-General, the latter in consultation with the appropriate United Nations agencies, take the following steps:

(*a*) Entrust the over-all responsibility for an agreed programme of environmental research at the international level to any central body that may be given the co-ordinating authority in the field of the environment, taking into account the co-ordination work already being provided on the regional level, especially by the Economic Commission for Europe;

(*b*) Identify, wherever possible, an existing agency within the United Nations system as the principal focal point for initiating and co-ordinating research in each principal area and, where there are competing claims, establish appropriate priorities;

(*c*) Designate the following as priority areas for research:
   (i)   Theories, policies and methods for the comprehensive environmental development of urban and rural settlements;
   (ii) Methods of assessing quantitative housing needs and of formulating and implementing phased programmes designed to satisfy them (principal bodies responsible: Department of Economic and Social Affairs of the United Nations Secretariat, regional economic commissions and United Nations Economic and Social Office in Beirut);
   (iii) Environmental socio-economic indicators of the quality of human settlements, particularly in terms of desirable occupancy standards and residential densities, with a view to identifying their time trends;
   (iv) Socio-economic and demographic factors underlying migration and spatial distribution of population, including the problem of transitional settlements (principal bodies responsible: Department of Economic and Social Affairs of the United Nations Secretariat (Centre for Housing, Building and Planning), United Nations Educational, Scientific and Cultural Organization, World Health Organization, International Labour Organization, Food and Agriculture Organization of the United Nations);
   (v)   Designs, technologies, financial and administrative procedures for the efficient and expanded production of housing and related infrastructure, suitably adapted to local conditions;
   (vi) Water supply, sewerage and waste-disposal systems adapted to local conditions, particularly in semi-tropical, tropical, Arctic and sub-Arctic areas (principal body responsible: World Health Organization);
   (vii) Alternative methods of meeting rapidly increasing urban transportation needs (principal bodies responsible: Department of Economic and Social Affairs of the United Nations Secretariat (Resources and Transport Division and Centre for Housing, Building and Planning));
   (viii) Physical, mental and social effects of stresses created by living and working conditions in human settlements, particularly urban conglomerates, for example the accessibility of buildings to persons whose physical mobility is impaired (principal bodies responsible: International Labour Organization, World Health Organization, United

Nations Educational, Scientific and Cultural Organization, Department of Economic and Social Affairs of the United Nations Secretariat).

2. *It is further recommended* that Governments consider co-operative arrangements to undertake the necessary research whenever the abov-mentioned problem areas have a specific regional impact. In such cases, provision should be made for the exchange of information and research findings with countries of other geographical regions sharing similar problems.

Recommendation 5

It is recommended:

(a) That Governments take steps to arrange for the exchange of visits by those who are conducting research in the public or private institutions of their countries;

(b) That Governments and the Secretary-General ensure the acceleration of the exchange of information concerning past and on-going research, experimentation and project implementation covering all aspects of human settlements, which is conducted by the United Nations system or by public or private entities including academic institutions.

Recommendation 6

It is recommended that Governments and the Secretary-General give urgent attention to the training of those who are needed to promote integrated action on the planning, development and management of human settlements.

Recommendation 7

It is recommended:

(a) That Governments and the Secretary-General provide equal possibilities for everybody, both by training and by ensuring access to relevant means and information, to influence their own environment by themselves;

(b) That Governments and the Secretary-General ensure that the institutions concerned shall be strengthened and that special training activities shall be established, making use of existing projects of regional environmental development, for the benefit of the less industrialized countries, covering the following:

(i) Intermediate and auxiliary personnel for national public services who, in turn, would be in a position to train others for similar tasks (principal bodies responsible: World Health Organization, Department of Economic and Social Affairs of the United Nations Secretariat (Centre for Housing, Building and Planning), United Nations Industrial Development Organization, Food and Agriculture Organization of the United Nations);

(ii) Specialists in environmental planning and in rural development (principal bodies responsible: Department of Economic and Social Affairs of the United Nations Secretariat (Centre for Housing, Building and Planning), Food and Agriculture Organization of the United Nations);

(iii) Community developers for self-help programmes for low-income groups (principal body responsible: Department of Economic and Social Affairs of the United Nations Secretariat (Centre for Housing, Building and Planning));

(iv) Specialists in working environments (principal bodies responsible: International Labour Organization, Department of Economic and Social Affairs of the United Nations Secretariat (Centre for Housing, Building and Planning), World Health Organization);

(v) Planners and organizers of mass transport systems and services with special reference to environmental development (principal body responsible: Department of Economic and Social Affairs of the United Nations Secretariat (Resources and Transport Division)).

Recommendation 8

It is recommended that regional institutions take stock of the requirements of their regions for various environmental skills and of the facilities available to meet those requirements in order to facilitate the provision of appropriate training within regions.

Recommendation 9

It is recommended that the World Health Organization increase its efforts to support Governments in planning for improving water supply and sewerage services through its community water supply programme, taking account, as far as possible, of the framework of total environment programmes for communities.

Recommendation 10

It is recommended that development assistance agencies should give higher priority, where justified in the light of the social benefits, to supporting Governments in financing and setting up services for water supply, disposal of water from all sources, and liquid-waste and solid-waste disposal and treatment as part of the objectives of the Second United Nations Development Decade.

Recommendation 11

It is recommended that the Secretary-General ensure that during the preparations for the 1970 World Population Conference, special attention shall be given to population concerns as they relate to the environment and, more particularly, to the environment of human settlements.

Recommendation 12

1. *It is recommended* that the World Health Organization and other United Nations agencies should provide increased assistance to Governments which so request in the field of family planning programmes without delay.

2. *It is further recommended* that the World Health Organization should promote and intensify research endeavour in the field of human reproduction, so that the serious consequences of population explosion on human environment can be prevented.

Recommendation 13

It is recommended that the United Nations agencies should focus special attention on the provision of assistance for combating the menace of human malnutrition rampant in many parts of the world. Such assistance will cover training, research and development endeavours on such matters as causes of malnutrition, mass production of high-protein and multipurpose foods, qualitative and quantitative characteristics of routine foods, and the launching of applied nutrition programmes.

Recommendation 14

It is recommended that the intergovernmental body for environmental affairs to be established within the United Nations should ensure that the required surveys shall be made concerning the need and the technical possibilities for developing internationally agreed standards and measuring and limiting noise emissions and that, if it is deemed advisable, such standards shall be applied in the production of means of transportation and certain kinds of working equipment, without a large price increase or reduction in the aid given to developing countries.

Recommendation 15

It is recommended that the Secretary-General, in consultation with the appropriate United Nations bodies, formulate programmes on a world-wide basis to assist countries to meet effectively the requirements of growth of human settlements and to improve the quality of life in existing settlements; in particular, in squatter areas.

Recommendation 16

The programmes referred to in recommendation 15 should include the establishment of subregional centres to undertake, *inter alia*, the following functions:

(a) Training;

(b) Research;

(c) Exchange of information;

(d) Financial, technical and material assistance.

Recommendation 17

It is recommended that Governments and the Secretary-General take immediate steps towards the establishment of an international fund or a financial institution whose primary operative objectives will be to assist in strengthening national programmes relating to human settlements through the provision of seed capital and the extension of the necessary technical assistance to permit an effective mobilization of domestic resources for housing and the environmental improvement of human settlements.

Recommendation 18

It is recommended that the following recommendations be referred to the Disaster Relief Co-ordinator for his consideration, more particularly in the context of the preparation of a report to the Economic and Social Council:

1. *It is recommended* that the Secretary-General, with the assistance of the Disaster Relief Co-ordinator and in consultation with the appropriate bodies of the United Nations system and non-governmental bodies:

(a) Assess the over-all requirements for the timely and widespread distribution of warnings which the observational and communications networks must satisfy;

(b) Assess the needs for additional observational networks and other observational systems for natural disaster detection and warnings for tropical storms (typhoons, hurricanes, cyclones etc.) and their associated storm surges, torrential rains, floods, tsunamis, earthquakes etc.;

(c) Evaluate the existing systems for the international communication of disaster warnings, in order to determine the extent to which these require improvement;

(d) On the basis of these assessments, promote, through existing national and international organizations, the establishment of an effective world-wide natural disaster warning system, with special emphasis on tropical cyclones and earthquakes, taking full advantage of existing systems and plans, such as the World Weather Watch, the World Meteorological Organization's Tropical Cyclone Project, the International Tsunami Warning System, the World-Wide Standardized Seismic Network and the Desert Locust Control Organization;

(e) Invite the World Meteorological Organization to promote research on the periodicity and intensity of the occurrence of droughts, with a view to developing improved forecasting techniques.

2. *It is further recommended* that the United Nations Development Programme and other appropriate international assistance agencies give priority in responding to requests from Governments for the establishment and improvement of natural disaster research programmes and warning systems.

3. *It is recommended* that the Secretary-General ensure that the United Nations system shall provide to Governments a comprehensive programme of advice and support in disaster prevention. More specifically, the question of disaster prevention should be seen as an integral part of the country programme as submitted to, and reviewed by, the United Nations Development Programme.

4. *It is recommended* that the Secretary-General take the necessary steps to ensure that the United Nations system shall assist countries with their planning for pre-disaster preparedness. To this end:

(a) An international programme of technical co-operation should be developed, designed to strengthen the capabilities of Governments in the field of pre-disaster planning, drawing upon the services of the resident representatives of the United Nations Development Programme;

(b) The Office of Disaster Relief, with the assistance of relevant agencies of the United Nations, should organize plans and programmes for international co-operation in cases of natural disasters;

(c) As appropriate, non-governmental international agencies and individual Governments should be invited to participate in the preparation of such plans and programmes.

ENVIRONMENTAL ASPECTS OF NATURAL RESOURCES MANAGEMENT

Recommendation 19

It is recommended that the Food and Agriculture Organization of the United Nations, in co-operation with other relevant international organizations, should include in its programme questions relating to rural planning in relation to environmental policy, since environmental policy is formulated in close association with physical planning and with medium-term and long-term economic and social planning. Even in highly industrialized countries, rural areas still cover more than 90 per cent of the territory and consequently should not be regarded as a residual sector and a mere reserve of land and manpower. The programme should therefore include, in particular:

(a) Arrangements for exchanges of such data as are available;

(b) Assistance in training and informing specialists and the public, especially young people, from primary school age onwards;

(c) The formulation of principles for the development of rural areas, which should be understood to comprise not only agricultural areas as such but also small- and medium-sized settlements and their hinterland.

Recommendation 20

It is recommended that the Food and Agriculture Organization of the United Nations, in co-operation with other international agencies concerned, strengthen the necessary machinery for the international acquisition of knowledge and transfer of experience on soil capabilities, degradation, conservation and restoration, and to this end:

(a) Co-operative information exchange should be facilitated among those nations sharing similar soils, climate and agricultural conditions;

  (i) The Soil Map of the World being prepared by the Food and Agriculture Organization of the United Nations, the United Nations Educational, Scientific and Cultural Organization and the International Society of Soil Science should serve to indicate those areas among which transfer of knowledge on soil potentialities and soil degradation and restoration would be most valuable;

  (ii) This map should be supplemented through the establishment of international criteria and methods for the assessment of soil capabilities and degradations and the collection of additional data based upon these methods and criteria. This should permit the preparation of a World Map of Soil Degradation Hazards as a framework for information exchange in this area;

  (iii) Information exchange on soil use should account for similarities in vegetation and other environmental conditions as well as those of soil, climate, and agricultural practices;

  (iv) The FAO Soil Data-Processing System should be developed beyond soil productivity considerations, to include the above-mentioned data and relevant environmental parameters, and to facilitate information exchange between national soil institutions, and eventually soil-monitoring stations;

(b) International co-operative research on soil capabilities and conservation should be strengthened and broadened to include:

  (i) Basic research on soil degradation processes in selected ecosystems under the auspices of the Man and the Biosphere Programme. This research should be directed as a matter of priority to those arid areas that are most threatened;

  (ii) Applied research on soil and water conservation practices under specific land-use conditions with the assistance of the Food and Agriculture Organization of the United Nations and, where appropriate, other agencies (United Nations Educational, Scientific and Cultural Organization, World Health Organization and International Atomic Energy Agency);

  (iii) Strengthening of existing research centres and, where necessary, establishment of new centres with the object of increasing the production from dry farming areas without any undue impairment of the environment;

  (iv) Research on the use of suitable soils for waste disposal and recycling; the United Nations Industrial Development Organization, the Food and Agriculture Organization of the United Nations, and the World Health Organization should enter into joint consultations regarding the feasibility of an international programme in this area;

(c) These efforts for international co-operation in research and information exchange on soils should be closely associated with those of the UNDP/WMO/FAO/UNESCO programme of agricultural biometeorology, in order to facilitate integration of data and practical findings and to support the national programmes of conservation of soil resources recommended above;

(d) It should moreover be noted that in addition to the various physical and climatic phenomena which contribute to soil degradation, economic and social factors contribute to it as well; among the economic contributory factors, one which should be particularly emphasized is the payment of inadequate prices for the agricultural produce of developing countries, which prevents farmers in those countries from setting aside sufficient savings for necessary investments in soil regeneration and conservation. Consequently, urgent remedial action should be taken by the organizations concerned to give new value and stability to the prices of raw materials of the developing countries.

Recommendation 21

It is recommended that Governments, the Food and Agriculture Organization of the United Nations and the World Health Organization, in co-operation with the United Nations Educational, Scientific and Cultural Organization and the International Atomic Energy Agency, strengthen and co-ordinate international programmes for integrated pest control and reduction of the harmful effects of agro-chemicals:

(*a*) Existing international activities for the exchange of information and co-operative research and technical assistance to developing countries should be strengthened to support the national programmes described above, with particular reference to:

(i) Basic research on ecological effects of pesticides and fertilizers (MAB);

(ii) Use of radio-isotope and radiation techniques in studying the fate of pesticides in the environment (joint IAEA/FAO Division);

(iii) Evaluation of the possibility of using pesticides of biological origin in substitution for certain chemical insecticides which cause serious disturbances in the environment;

(iv) Dose and timing of fertilizers' application and their effects on soil productivity and the environment (Food and Agriculture Organization of the United Nations);

(v) Management practices and techniques for integrated pest control, including biological control (Food and Agriculture Organization of the United Nations and World Health Organization);

(vi) Establishment and/or strengthening of national and regional centres for integrated pest control, particularly in developing countries (Food and Agriculture Organization of the United Nations and World Health Organization);

(*b*) Existing expert committees of the Food and Agriculture Organization of the United Nations and the World Health Organization on various aspects of pest control should be convened periodically:

(i) To assess recent advances in the relevant fields of research mentioned above;

(ii) To review and further develop international guidelines and standards with special reference to national and ecological conditions in relation to the use of chlorinated hydrocarbons, pesticides containing heavy metals and the use and experimentation of biological controls;

(*c*) In addition, *ad hoc* panels of experts should be convened, by the Food and Agriculture Organization of the United Nations, the World Health Organization and, where appropriate, the International Atomic Energy Agency, in order to study specific problems, and facilitate the work of the above-mentioned committees.

Recommendation 22

It is recommended that the Food and Agriculture Organization of the United

Nations, under its "War on Waste" programme, place increased emphasis on control and recycling of wastes in agriculture:

(a) This programme should assist the national activities relating to:
  (i) Control and recycling of crop residues and animal wastes;
  (ii) Control and recycling of agro-industrial waste;
  (iii) Use of municipal wastes as fertilizers;

(b) The programme should also include measures to avoid wasteful use of natural resources through the destruction of unmarketable agricultural products or their use for improper purposes.

Recommendation 23

It is recommended that Governments, in co-operation with the Food and Agriculture Organization of the United Nations and other agencies and bodies, establish and strengthen regional and international machinery for the rapid development and management of domesticated livestock of economic importance and their related environmental aspects as part of the ecosystems, particularly in areas of low annual productivity, and thus encourage the establishment of regional livestock research facilities, councils and commissions, as appropriate.

Recommendation 24

It is recommended that the Secretary-General take steps to ensure that the United Nations bodies concerned co-operate to meet the needs for new knowledge on the environmental aspects of forests and forest management:

(a) Where appropriate, research should be promoted, assisted, co-ordinated, or undertaken by the Man and the Biosphere Programme (UNESCO), in close co-operation with the Food and Agriculture Organization of the United Nations and the World Meteorological Organization, and with the collaboration of the International Council of Scientific Unions and the International Union of Forestry Research Organizations;

(b) Research on comparative legislation, land tenure, institutions, tropical forest management, the effects of the international trade in forest products on national forest environments, and public administration, should be sponsored or co-ordinated by FAO, in co-operation with other appropriate international and regional organizations;

(c) The Food and Agriculture Organization of the United Nations, in conjunction with the United Nations Educational, Scientific and Cultural Organization and other appropriate international organizations, should give positive advice to member countries on the important role of forests with reference to, and in conjunction with, the conservation of soil, watersheds, the protection of tourist sites and wildlife, and recreation, within the over-all framework of the interests of the biosphere.

Recommendation 25

It is recommended that the Secretary-General take steps to ensure that continuing surveillance, with the co-operation of Member States, of the world's forest cover shall be provided for through the programmes of the Food and Agriculture Organization of the United Nations and the United Nations Educational, Scientific and Cultural Organization.

(a) Such a World Forest Appraisal Programme would provide basic data, including data on the balance between the world's forest biomass and the prevailing environment, and changes in the forest biomass, considered to have a significant impact on the environment;

(*b*)   The information could be collected from existing inventories and on-going activities and through remote-sensing techniques;

(*c*)   The forest protection programme described above might be incorporated within this effort, through the use of advanced technology, such as satellites which use different types of imagery and which could constantly survey all forests.

Recommendation 26

It is recommended that the Food and Agriculture Organization of the United Nations co-ordinate an international programme for research and exchange of information on forest fires, pests and diseases:

(*a*)   The programme should include data collection and dissemination, identification of potentially susceptible areas and of means of suppression; exchange of information on technologies, equipment and techniques; research, including integrated pest control and the influence of fires on forest ecosystems, to be undertaken by the International Union of Forestry Research Organizations; establishment of a forecasting system in co-operation with the World Meteorological Organization; organization of seminars and study tours; the facilitation of bilateral agreements for forest protection between neighbouring countries, and the development of effective international quarantines;

(*b*)   Forest fires, pests and diseases will frequently each require separate individual treatment.

Recommendation 27

It is recommended that the Food and Agriculture Organization of the United Nations facilitate the transfer of information on forests and forest management:

(*a*)   The amount of knowledge that can usefully be exchanged is limited by the differences of climatic zones and forest types;

(*b*)   The exchange of information should however be encouraged among nations sharing similarities; considerable knowledge is already exchanged among the industrialized nations of the temperate zone;

(*c*)   Opportunities exist, despite differences, for the useful transfer of information to developing countries on the environmental aspects of such items as: (i) the harvesting and industrialization of some tropical hardwoods; (ii) pine cultures; (iii) the principles of forest management systems and management science; (iv) soils and soil interpretations relating to forest management; (v) water régimes and watershed management; (vi) forest industries pollution controls, including both technical and economic data; (vii) methods for the evaluation of forest resources through sampling techniques, remote sensing, and data-processing; (viii) control of destructive fires and pest outbreaks; and (ix) co-ordination in the area of the definition and standardization of criteria and methods for the economic appraisal of forest environmental influences and for the comparison of alternative uses.

Recommendation 28

It is recommended that the Food and Agriculture Organization of the United Nations strengthen its efforts in support of forestry projects and research projects, possibly for production, in finding species which are adaptable even in areas where this is exceptionally difficult because of ecological conditions.

Recommendation 29

It is recommended that the Secretary-General ensure that the effect of pollutants upon wildlife shall be considered, where appropriate, within environmental monitoring systems. Particular attention should be paid to those species of wildlife that may serve as indicators for future wide environmental disturbances, and an ultimate impact upon human populations.

Recommendation 30

It is recommended that the Secretary-General ensure the establishment of a programme to expand present data-gathering processes so as to assess the total economic value of wildlife resources.

(*a*) Such data would facilitate the task of monitoring the current situation of animals endangered by their trade value, and demonstrate to questioning nations the value of their resources;

(*b*) Such a programme should elaborate upon current efforts of the Food and Agriculture Organization of the United Nations and might well produce a yearbook of wildlife[1] statistics.

Recommendation 31

It is recommended that the Secretary-General ensure that the appropriate United Nations agencies co-operate with the Governments of the developing countries to develop special short-term training courses on wildlife[1] management:

(*a*) Priority should be given to conversion courses for personnel trained in related disciplines such as forestry or animal husbandry;

(*b*) Special attention should be given to the establishment and support of regional training schools for technicians.

Recommendation 32

It is recommended that Governments give attention to the need to enact international conventions and treaties to protect species inhabiting international waters or those which migrate from one country to another:

(*a*) A broadly-based convention should be considered which would provide a framework by which criteria for game regulations could be agreed upon and the over-exploitation of resources curtailed by signatory countries;

(*b*) A working group should be set up as soon as possible by the appropriate authorities to consider these problems and to advise on the need for, and possible scope of, such conventions or treaties.

Recommendation 33

It is recommended that Governments agree to strengthen the international whaling commission, to increase international research efforts, and as a matter of urgency to call for an international agreement, under the auspices of the international whaling commission and involving all Governments concerned, for a 10-year moratorium on commercial whaling.

Recommendation 34

It is recommended that Governments and the Secretary-General give special attention to training requirements on the management of parks and protected areas:

(*a*) High-level training should be provided and supported:

---

1. Whereas elsewhere in this report the expression "wildlife" is meant to include both animals and plants, it should be understood here to be restricted to the most important animals.

(i) In addition to integrating aspects of national parks planning and management into courses on forestry and other subjects, special degrees
should be offered in park management; the traditional forestry, soil and
geology background of the park manager must be broadened into an
integrated approach;

(ii) Graduate courses in natural resources administration should be made
available in at least one major university in every continent;

(b) Schools offering courses in national park management at a medium-grade
level should be assisted by the establishment or expansion of facilities, particularly
in Latin America and Asia.

Recommendation 35

It is recommended that the Secretary-General take steps to ensure that an appropriate mechanism shall exist for the exchange of information on national parks
legislation and planning and management techniques developed in some countries
which could serve as guidelines to be made available to any interested country.

Recommendation 36

It is recommended that the Secretary-General take steps to ensure that the appropriate United Nations agencies shall assist the developing countries to plan for the
inflow of visitors into their protected areas in such a way as to reconcile revenue
and environmental considerations within the context of the recommendations
approved by the Conference. The other international organizations concerned may
likewise make their contribution.

Recommendation 37

It is recommended that Governments take steps to co-ordinate, and co-operate in
the management of, neighbouring or contiguous protected areas. Agreement should
be reached on such aspects as mutual legislation, patrolling systems, exchange of
information, research projects, collaboration on measures of burning, plant and
animal control, fishery regulations, censuses, tourist circuits and frontier formalities.

Recommendation 38

It is recommended that Governments take steps to set aside areas representing
ecosystems of international significance for protection under international agreement.

Recommendation 39

It is recommended that Governments, in co-operation with the Secretary-General
of the United Nations and the Food and Agriculture Organization of the United
Nations where indicated, agree to an international programme to preserve the
world's genetic resources:

(a) Active participation at the national and international levels is involved. It
must be recognized, however, that while survey, collection, and dissemination of
these genetic resources are best carried out on a regional or international basis, their
actual evaluation and utilization are matters for specific institutions and individual
workers; international participation in the latter should concern exchange of techniques and findings;

(b) An international network is required with appropriate machinery to facilitate the interchange of information and genetic material among countries;

(c) Both static (seed banks, culture collection etc.) and dynamic (conservation of
populations in evolving natural environments) ways are needed.

(*d*) Action is necessary in six interrelated areas:
  (i) Survey of genetic resources;
  (ii) Inventory of collections;
  (iii) Exploration and collecting;
  (iv) Documentation;
  (v) Evaluation and utilization;
  (vi) Conservation, which represents the crucial element to which all other programmes relate;

(*e*) Although the international programme relates to all types of genetic resources, the action required for each resource will vary according to existing needs and activities.

Recommendation 40

It is recommended that Governments, in co-operation with the Secretary-General of the United Nations and the Food and Agriculture Organization of the United Nations where indicated, make inventories of the genetic resources most endangered by depletion or extinction:

(*a*) All species threatened by man's development should be included in such inventories;

(*b*) Special attention should be given to locating in this field those areas of natural genetic diversity that are disappearing;

(*c*) These inventories should be reviewed periodically and brought up to date by appropriate monitoring;

(*d*) The survey conducted by FAO in collaboration with the International Biological Programme is designed to provide information on endangered crop genetic resources by 1972, but will require extension and follow-up.

Recommendation 41

It is recommended that Governments, in co-operation with the Secretary-General of the United Nations and the Food and Agriculture Organization of the United Nations where indicated, compile or extend, as necessary, registers of existing collections of genetic resources:

(*a*) Such registers should identify which breeding and experiment stations, research institutions and universities maintain which collections;

(*b*) Major gaps in existing collections should be identified where material is in danger of being lost;

(*c*) These inventories of collections should be transformed for computer handling and made available to all potential users;

(*d*) In respect of plants:
  (i) It would be expected that the "advanced varieties" would be well represented, but that primitive materials would be found to be scarce and require subsequent action;
  (ii) The action already initiated by FAO, several national institutions, and international foundations should be supported and expanded.

(*e*) In respect of micro-organisms, it is recommended that each nation develop comprehensive inventories of culture collections:
  (i) A cataloguing of the large and small collections and the value of their holdings is required, rather than a listing of individual strains;
  (ii) Many very small but unique collections, sometimes the works of a single specialist, are lost;

(iii)   Governments should make sure that valuable gene pools held by individuals or small institutes are also held in national or regional collections.

(f)   In respect of animal germ plasm, it is recommended that FAO establish a continuing mechanism to assess and maintain catalogues of the characteristics of domestic animal breeds, types and varieties in all nations of the world. Likewise, FAO should establish such lists where required.

(g)   In respect of aquatic organisms, it is recommended that FAO compile a catalogue of genetic resources of cultivated species and promote intensive studies on the methods of preservation and storage of genetic material.

Recommendation 42

It is recommended that Governments, in co-operation with the Secretary-General of the United Nations and the Food and Agriculture Organization of the United Nations where indicated, initiate immediately, in co-operation with all interested parties, programmes of exploration and collection wherever endangered species have been identified which are not included in existing collections:

(a)   An emergency programme, with the co-operation of the Man and the Biosphere Programme, of plant exploration and collection should be launched on the basis of the FAO List of Emergency Situations for a five-year period;

(b)   With regard to forestry species, in addition to the efforts of the Danish/ FAO Forest Tree Seed Centre, the International Union of Forestry Research Organizations, and the FAO Panel of Experts on Forest Gene Resources, support is needed for missions planned for Latin America, West Africa, the East Indies and India.

Recommendation 43

It is recommended that Governments, in co-operation with the Secretary-General of the United Nations and the Food and Agriculture Organization of the United Nations where indicated:

1.   Recognize that conservation is a most crucial part of any genetic resources programme. Moreover, major types of genetic resources must be treated separately because:

(a)   They are each subject to different programmes and priorities;

(b)   They serve different uses and purposes;

(c)   They require different expertise, techniques and facilities;

2.   In respect of plant germ plasms (agriculture and forestry), organize and equip national or regional genetic resources conservation centres:

(a)   Such centres as the National Seed Storage Laboratory in the United States of America and the Vavilov Institute of Plant Industry in the Union of Soviet Socialist Republics already provide good examples;

(b)   Working collections should be established separately from the basic collections; these will usually be located at plant and breeding stations and will be widely distributed;

(c)   Three classes of genetic crop resources must be conserved:
   (i)   High-producing varieties in current use and those they have superseded;
   (ii)   Primitive varieties of traditional pre-scientific agriculture (recognized as genetic treasuries for plan improvements);
   (iii)   Mutations induced by radiation or chemical means;

(*d*) Species contributing to environmental improvement, such as sedge used to stabilize sand-dunes, should be conserved;

(*e*) Wild or weed relatives of crop species and those wild species of actual or potential use in rangelands, industry, new crops etc. should be included;

3. In respect of plant germ plasms (agriculture and forestry), maintain gene pools of wild plant species within their natural communities. Therefore:

(*a*) It is essential that primeval forests, bushlands and grasslands which contain important forest genetic resources be identified and protected by appropriate technical and legal means; systems of reserves exist in most countries, but a strengthening of international understanding on methods of protection and on availability of material may be desired;

(*b*) Conservation of species of medical, aesthetic or research value should be assured;

(*c*) The network of biological reserves proposed by UNESCO (Man and the Biosphere Programme) should be designed, where feasible, to protect these natural communities;

(*d*) Where protection in nature becomes uncertain or impossible, then means such as seed storage or living collections in provenance trials or botanic gardens must be adopted;

4. Fully implement the programmes initiated by the FAO Panels of Experts on forest gene resources in 1968 and on plant exploration and introduction in 1970;

5. In respect of animal germ plasm, consider the desirability and feasibility of international action to preserve breeds or varieties of animals:

(*a*) Because such an endeavour would constitute a major effort beyond the scope of any one nation, FAO would be the logical executor of such a project. Close co-operation with Governments would be necessary, however. The International Union for Conservation of Nature and Natural Resources might, logically, be given responsibility for wild species, in co-operation with FAO, the Man and the Biosphere Programme (UNESCO), and Governments.

(*b*) Any such effort should also include research on methods of preserving, storing, and transporting germ plasm;

(*c*) Specific methods for the maintenance of gene pools of aquatic species should be developed;

(*d*) The recommendations of the FAO Working Party Meeting on Genetic Selection and Conservation of Genetic Resources of Fish, held in 1971, should be implemented;

6. In respect of micro-organism germ plasms, co-operatively establish and properly fund a few large regional collections:

(*a*) Full use should be made of major collections now in existence;

(*b*) In order to provide geographical distribution and access to the developing nations, regional centres should be established in Africa, Asia and Latin America and the existing centres in the developed world should be strengthened;

7. Establish conservation centres of insect germ plasm. The very difficult and long process of selecting or breeding insects conducive to biological control programmes can begin only in this manner.

Recommendation 44

It is recommended that Governments, in co-operation with the Secretary-General of the United Nations and the Food and Agriculture Organization of the United

Nations where indicated, recognize that evaluation and utilization are critical corollaries to the conservation of genetic resources. In respect of crop-breeding programmes, it is recommended that Governments give special emphasis to:

(a) The quality of varieties and breeds and the potential for increased yields;

(b) The ecological conditions to which the species are adapted;

(c) The resistance to diseases, pests and other adverse factors;

(d) The need for a multiplicity of efforts so as to increase the chances of success.

Recommendation 45

It is recommended that Governments, in co-operation with the Secretary-General of the United Nations and the Food and Agriculture Organization of the United Nations where indicated:

1. Collaborate to establish a global network of national and regional institutes relating to genetic resource conservation based on agreements on the availability of material and information, on methods, on technical standards, and on the need for technical and financial assistance wherever required:

(a) Facilities should be designed to assure the use of the materials and information: (i) by breeders, to develop varieties and breeds both giving higher yields and having higher resistance to local pests and diseases and other adverse factors; and (ii) by users providing facilities and advice for the safest and most profitable utilization of varieties and breeds most adapted to local conditions;

(b) Such co-operation would apply to all genetic resource conservation centres and to all types mentioned in the foregoing recommendations;

(c) Standardized storage and retrieval facilities for the exchange of information and genetic material should be developed:

(i) Information should be made generally available and its exchange facilitated through agreement on methods and technical standards;

(ii) International standards and regulations for the shipment of materials should be agreed upon;

(iii) Basic collections and data banks should be replicated in at least two distinct sites, and should remain a national responsibility;

(iv) A standardized and computerized system of documentation is required;

(d) Technical and financial assistance should be provided where required; areas of genetic diversity are most frequently located in those countries most poorly equipped to institute the necessary programmes;

2. Recognize that the need for liaison among the parties participating in the global system of genetic resources conservation requires certain institutional innovations. To this end:

(a) *It is recommended* that the appropriate United Nations agency establish an international liaison unit for plant genetic resources in order:

(i) To improve liaison between governmental and non-governmental efforts;

(ii) To assist in the liaison and co-operation between national and regional centres, with special emphasis on international agreements on methodology and standards of conservation of genetic material, standardization and co-ordination of computerized record systems, and the exchange of information and material between such centres;

(iii) To assist in implementing training courses in exploration, conservation and breeding methods and techniques;

(iv) To act as a central repository for copies of computerized information on gene pools (discs and tapes);

(v) To provide the secretariat for periodic meetings of international panels and seminars on the subject; a conference on germ plasm conservation might be convened to follow up the successful conference of 1967;

(vi) To plan and co-ordinate the five-year emergency programme on the conservation of endangered species;

(vii) To assist Governments further, wherever required, in implementing their national programmes;

(viii) To promote the evaluation and utilization of genetic resources at the national and international levels;

(b) *It is recommended* that the appropriate United Nations agency initiate the required programme on micro-organism germ plasm:

(i) Periodic international conferences involving those concerned with the maintenance of and research on gene pools of micro-organisms should be supported;

(ii) Such a programme might interact with the proposed regional culture centres by assuring that each centre places high priority on the training of scientists and technicians from the developing nations; acting as a necessary liaison; and lending financial assistance to those countries established outside the developed countries;

(iii) The international exchange of pure collections of micro-organisms between the major collections of the world has operated for many years and requires little re-enforcement;

(iv) Study should be conducted particularly on waste disposal and recycling, controlling diseases and pests, and food technology and nutrition;

(c) *It is recommended* that the Food and Agriculture Organization of the United Nations institute a programme in respect of animal germ plasm to assess and maintain catalogues of the economic characteristics of domestic animal breeds and types and of wild species and to establish gene pools of potentially useful types;

(d) *It is recommended* that the Man and the Biosphere project on the conservation of natural areas and the genetic material contained therein should be adequately supported.

Recommendation 46

It is recommended that Governments, and the Secretary-General in co-operation with the Food and Agriculture Organization of the United Nations and other United Nations organizations concerned, as well as development assistance agencies, take steps to support recent guidelines, recommendations and programmes of the various international fishing organizations. A large part of the needed international action has been identified with action programmes initiated by FAO and its Intergovernmental Committee on Fisheries and approximately 24 other bilateral and multilateral international commissions, councils and committees. In particular these organizations are planning and undertaking:

(a) Co-operative programmes such as that of LEPOR (Long-Term and Expanded Programme of Oceanic Research), GIPME (Global Investigation of Pollution in the Marine Environment) and IBP (International Biological Programme);

(b) Exchange of data, supplementing and expanding the services maintained by FAO and bodies within its framework in compiling, disseminating and co-ordinating information on living aquatic resources and their environment and fisheries activities;

(*c*) Evaluation and monitoring of world fishery resources, environmental conditions, stock assessment, including statistics on catch and effort, and the economics of fisheries;

(*d*) Assistance to Governments in interpreting the implications of such assessments, identifying alternative management measures, and formulating required actions;

(*e*) Special programmes and recommendations for management of stocks of fish and other aquatic animals proposed by the existing international fishery bodies. Damage to fish stocks has often occurred because regulatory action is taken too slowly. In the past, the need for management action to be nearly unanimous has reduced action to the minimum acceptable level.

Recommendation 47

It is recommended that Governments, and the Secretary-General of the United Nations in co-operation with the Food and Agriculture Organization of the United Nations and other United Nations organizations concerned, as well as development assistance agencies, take steps to ensure close participation of fishery agencies and interests in the preparations for the United Nations Conference on the Law of the Sea. In order to safeguard the marine environment and its resources through the development of effective and workable principles and laws, the information and insight of international and regional fishery bodies, as well as the national fishery agencies are essential.

Recommendation 48

It is recommended that Governments, and the Secretary-General in co-operation with the Food and Agriculture Organization of the United Nations and other United Nations organizations concerned, as well as development assistance agencies, take steps to ensure international co-operation in the research, control and regulation of the side effects of national activities in resource utilization where these affect the aquatic resources of other nations:

(*a*) Estuaries, intertidal marshes, and other near-shore and in-shore environments play a crucial role in the maintenance of several marine fish stocks. Similar problems exist in those fresh-water fisheries that occur in shared waters;

(*b*) Discharge of toxic chemicals, heavy metals, and other wastes may affect even high-seas resources;

(*c*) Certain exotic species, notably the carp, lamprey and alewife, have invaded international waters with deleterious effects as a result of unregulated unilateral action.

Recommendation 49

It is recommended that Governments, and the Secretary-General of the United Nations in co-operation with the Food and Agriculture Organization of the United Nations and other United Nations organizations concerned, as well as development assistance agencies, take steps to develop further and strengthen facilities for collecting, analysing and disseminating data on living aquatic resources and the environment in which they live:

(*a*) Data already exist concerning the total harvest from the oceans and from certain regions in respect of individual fish stocks, their quantity, and the fishing efforts expended on them, and in respect of their population structure, distribution and changes. This coverage needs to be improved and extended;

(b) It is clear that a much greater range of biological parameters must be monitored and analysed in order to provide an adequate basis for evaluating the interaction of stocks and managing the combined resources of many stocks. There is no institutional constraint on this expansion but a substantial increase in funding is needed by FAO and other international organizations concerned to meet this expanding need for data;

(c) Full utilization of present and expanded data facilities is dependent on the co-operation of Governments in developing local and regional data networks, making existing data available to FAO and to the international bodies, and formalizing the links between national and international agencies responsible for monitoring and evaluating fishery resources.

Recommendation 50

It is recommended that Governments, and the Secretary-General of the United Nations in co-operation with the Food and Agriculture Organization of the United Nations and other United Nations organizations concerned, as well as development assistance agencies, take steps to ensure full co-operation among Governments by strengthening the existing international and regional machinery for development and management of fisheries and their related environmental aspects and, in those regions where these do not exist, to encourage the establishment of fishery councils and commissions as appropriate.

(a) The operational efficiency of these bodies will depend largely on the ability of the participating countries to carry out their share of the activities and programmes;

(b) Technical support and servicing from the specialized agencies, in particular from FAO, is also required;

(c) The assistance of bilateral and international funding agencies will be needed to ensure the full participation of the developing countries in these activities.

Recommendation 51

It is recommended that Governments concerned consider the creation of river-basin commissions or other appropriate machinery for co-operation between interested States for water resources common to more than one jurisdiction.

(a) In accordance with the Charter of the United Nations and the principles of international law full consideration must be given to the right of permanent sovereignty of each country concerned to develop its own resources;

(b) The following principles should be considered by the States concerned when appropriate:

    (i) Nations agree that when major water resource activities are contemplated that may have a significant environmental effect on another country, the other country should be notified well in advance of the activity envisaged;

    (ii) The basic objective of all water resource use and development activities from the environmental point of view is to ensure the best use of water and to avoid its pollution in each country;

    (iii) The net benefits of hydrologic regions common to more than one national jurisdiction are to be shared equitably by the nations affected;

(c)   Such arrangements, when deemed appropriate by the States concerned, will permit undertaking on a regional basis:

    (i)   Collection, analysis, and exchanges of hydrologic data through some international mechanism agreed upon by the States concerned;

    (ii)   Joint data-collection programmes to serve planning needs;

    (iii)   Assessment of environmental effects of existing water uses;

    (iv)   Joint study of the causes and symptoms of problems related to water resources, taking into account the technical, economic, and social considerations of water quality control;

    (v)   Rational use, including a programme of quality control, of the water resource as an environmental asset;

    (vi)   Provision for the judicial and administrative protection of water rights and claims;

    (vii)   Prevention and settlement of disputes with reference to the management and conservation of water resources;

    (viii)   Financial and technical co-operation of a shared resource;

(d)   Regional conferences should be organized to promote the above considerations.

Recommendation 52

It is recommended that the Secretary-General take steps to ensure that appropriate United Nations bodies support government action where required:

1.   Reference is made to the Food and Agriculture Organization of the United Nations, the World Health Organization, the World Meteorological Organization, the Department of Economic and Social Affairs of the United Nations Secretariat (Resources and Transport Division), the United Nations Educational, Scientific and Cultural Organization/International Hydrological Decade, the regional economic commissions and the United Nations Economic and Social Office in Beirut. For example:

(a)   The Food and Agriculture Organization of the United Nations has established a Commission on Land and Water Use for the Middle East which promotes regional co-operation in research, training and information, *inter alia* on water management problems;

(b)   The World Health Organization has available the International Reference Centre for Waste Disposal located at Dübendorf, Switzerland, and International Reference Centre on Community Water Supply in the Netherlands;

(c)   The World Meteorological Organization has a Commission on Hydrology which provides guidance on data collection and on the establishment of hydrological networks;

(d)   The Resources and Transport Division of the Department of Economic and Social Affairs, United Nations Secretariat, has the United Nations Water Resources Development Centre;

(e)   The United Nations Educational, Scientific and Cultural Organization is sponsoring the International Hydrological Decade programme of co-ordinated research on the quality and quantity of world water resources.

2.   Similar specialized centres should be established at the regional level in developing countries for training research and information exchange on:

(a)   Inland water pollution and waste disposal in co-operation with the World Health Organization, the Food and Agriculture Organization of the United Nations, the United Nations regional economic commissions and the United Nations Economic and Social Office in Beirut;

(b)   Water management for rain-fed and irrigated agriculture, by the Food and Agriculture Organization of the United Nations in co-operation with the regional economic commissions and the United Nations Economic and Social Office in Beirut;

(c)   Integrated water resources planning and management in co-operation with the Department of Economic and Social Affairs of the United Nations Secretariat (Resources and Transport Division), the regional economic commissions, and the United Nations Economic and Social Office in Beirut.

Recommendation 53

It is recommended that the Secretary-General take steps to ensure that the United Nations system is prepared to provide technical and financial assistance to Governments when requested in the different functions of water resources management:

(a)   Surveys and inventories;

(b)   Water resources administration and policies, including:

   (i)   The establishment of institutional frameworks;

   (ii)   Economic structures of water resources management and development;

   (iii)   Water resources law and legislation;

(c)   Planning and management techniques, including:

   (i)   The assignment of water quality standards;

   (ii)   The implementation of appropriate technology;

   (iii)   More efficient use and re-use of limited water supplies;

(d)   Basic and applied studies and research;

(e)   Transfer of existing knowledge;

(f)   Continuing support of the programme of the International Hydrological Decade.

Recommendation 54

It is recommended that the Secretary-General take steps to establish a roster of experts who would be available to assist Governments, upon request, to anticipate and evaluate the environmental effects of major water development projects. Governments would have the opportunity of consulting teams of experts drawn from this roster, in the first stages of project planning. Guidelines could be prepared to assist in the review and choices of alternatives.

Recommendation 55

It is recommended that the Secretary-General take steps to conduct an exploratory programme to assess the actual and potential environmental effects of water management upon the oceans, define terms and estimate the costs for a comprehensive programme of action, and establish and maintain as far as possible:

(a)   A world registry of major or otherwise important rivers arranged regionally and classified according to their discharge of water and pollutants;

(b)   A world registry of clean rivers which would be defined in accordance with internationally agreed quality criteria and to which nations would contribute on a voluntary basis:

   (i)   The oceans are the ultimate recipient for the natural and man-made wastes discharged into the river systems of the continents;

   (ii)   Changes in the amount of river-flow into the oceans, as well as in its distribution in space and time, may considerably affect the physical, chemical and biological régime of the estuary regions and influence the oceanic water systems;

(iii) It would be desirable for nations to declare their intention to have admitted to the world registry of clean rivers those rivers within their jurisdiction that meet the quality criteria as defined and to declare their further intention to ensure that certain other rivers shall meet those quality criteria by some target date.

Recommendation 56

It is recommended that the Secretary-General provide the appropriate vehicle for the exchange of information on mining and mineral processing.

(a) Improved accessibility and dissemination of existing information is required; the body of literature and experience is already larger than one would think.

(b) Possibilities include the accumulation of information on: (i) the environmental conditions of mine sites; (ii) the action taken in respect of the environment; and (iii) the positive and negative environmental repercussions.

(c) Such a body of information could be used for prediction. Criteria for the planning and management of mineral production would emerge and would indicate where certain kinds of mining should be limited, where reclamation costs would be particularly high, or where other problems would arise.

(d) The appropriate United Nations bodies should make efforts to assist the developing countries by, *inter alia*, providing adequate information for each country on the technology for preventing present or future environmentally adverse effects of mining and the adverse health and safety effects associated with the mineral industry, and by accepting technical trainees and sending experts.

Recommendation 57

It is recommended that the Secretary-General take steps to ensure proper collection, measurement and analysis of data relating to the environmental effects of energy use and production within appropriate monitoring systems.

(a) The design and operation of such networks should include, in particular, monitoring the environmental levels resulting from emission of carbon dioxide, sulphur dioxide, oxidants, nitrogen oxides (NO_x), heat and particulates, as well as those from releases of oil and radioactivity;

(b) In each case the objective is to learn more about the relationships between such levels and the effects on weather, human health, plant and animal life, and amenity values.

Recommendation 58

It is recommended that the Secretary-General take steps to give special attention to providing a mechanism for the exchange of information on energy:

(a) The rationalization and integration of resource management for energy will clearly require a solid understanding of the complexity of the problem and of the multiplicity of alternative solutions;

(b) Access to the large body of existing information should be facilitated:
  (i) Data on the environmental consequences of different energy systems should be provided through an exchange of national experiences, studies, seminars, and other appropriate meetings;
  (ii) A continually updated register of research involving both entire systems and each of its stages should be maintained.

Recommendation 59

It is recommended that the Secretary-General take steps to ensure that a comprehensive study be promptly undertaken with the aim of submitting a first report, at the latest in 1975, on available energy sources, new technology, and consumption trends, in order to assist in providing a basis for the most effective development of the world's energy resources, with due regard to the environmental effects of energy production and use; such a study to be carried out in collaboration with appropriate international bodies such as the International Atomic Energy Agency and the Organization for Economic Co-operation and Development.

Recommendation 60

It is recommended that the Secretary-General, in co-operation with Governments concerned and the appropriate international agencies, arrange for systematic audits of natural resource development projects in representative ecosystems of international significance to be undertaken jointly with the Governments concerned after, and where feasible before, the implementation of such projects.[2]

Recommendation 61

It is recommended that the Secretary-General, in co-operation with Governments concerned and the appropriate international agencies, provide that pilot studies be conducted in representative ecosystems of international significance to assess the environmental impact of alternative approaches to the survey, planning and development of resource projects.

Recommendation 62

It is recommended that the Secretary-General, in co-operation with Governments concerned and the appropriate international agencies, provide that studies be conducted to find out the connexion between the distribution of natural resources and people's welfare and the reasons for possible discrepancies.

Recommendation 63

It is recommended that the Secretary-General take steps to ensure that international development assistance agencies, in co-operation with recipient Governments, intensify efforts to revise and broaden the criteria of development project analysis to incorporate environmental impact considerations.

Recommendation 64

It is recommended that the Secretary-General take steps to ensure that the United Nations agencies concerned undertake studies on the relative costs and benefits of synthetic *versus* natural products serving identical uses.

Recommendation 65

It is recommended that the Man and the Biosphere Programme be vigorously pursued by the United Nations Educational, Scientific and Cultural Organization

---

2. Projects might include new agricultural settlement of subtropical and tropical zones, irrigation and drainage in arid zones, tropical forestry development, major hydroelectric developments, land reclamation works in tropical lowland coastal areas, and settlement of nomads in semi-arid zones. The cost of audits in developing countries should not be imputed to the costs of the resource development projects but financed from separate international sources.

in co-operation with other United Nations organizations and other international scientific organizations.

Recommendation 66

It is recommended that the World Meteorological Organization initiate or intensify studies on the interrelationships of resource development and meteorology.

Recommendation 67

It is recommended that the Secretary-General, in co-operation with interested Governments and United Nations specialized agencies, take the necessary steps to encourage the further development of remote-sensing techniques for resources surveys and the utilization of these techniques on the basis of proper international arrangements.

Recommendation 68

It is recommended that the Secretary-General, in co-operation with the appropriate agencies of the United Nations and other international organizations, promote jointly with interested Governments the development of methods for the integrated planning and management of natural resources, and provide, when requested, advice to Governments on such methods, in accordance with the particular environmental circumstances of each country.

Recommendation 69

It is recommended that the Food and Agriculture Organization of the United Nations expand its present programme on the stabilization of marginal lands.

Identification and control of pollutants of broad international significance

A. POLLUTION GENERALLY

Recommendation 70

It is recommended that Governments be mindful of activities in which there is an appreciable risk of effects on climate, and to this end:

(*a*) Carefully evaluate the likelihood and magnitude of climatic effects and disseminate their findings to the maximum extent feasible before embarking on such activities;

(*b*) Consult fully other interested States when activities carrying a risk of such effects are being contemplated or implemented.

Recommendation 71

It is recommended that Governments use the best practicable means available to minimize the release to the environment of toxic or dangerous substances, especially if they are persistent substances such as heavy metals and organochlorine compounds, until it has been demonstrated that their release will not give rise to unacceptable risks or unless their use is essential to human health or food production, in which case appropriate control measures should be applied.

Recommendation 72

It is recommended that in establishing standards for pollutants of international significance, Governments take into account the relevant standards proposed by competent international organizations, and concert with other concerned Governments and the competent international organizations in planning and carrying out control programmes for pollutants distributed beyond the national jurisdiction from which they are released.

Recommendation 73

It is recommended that Governments actively support, and contribute to, international programmes to acquire knowledge for the assessment of pollutant sources, pathways, exposures and risks and that those Governments in a position to do so provide educational, technical and other forms of assistance to facilitate broad participation by countries regardless of their economic or technical advancement.

Recommendation 74

It is recommended that the Secretary-General, drawing on the resources of the entire United Nations system, and with the active support of Governments and appropriate scientific and other international bodies:

(*a*) Increase the capability of the United Nations system to provide awareness and advance warning of deleterious effects to human health and well-being from man-made pollutants;

(*b*) Provide this information in a form which is useful to policy-makers at the national level;

(*c*) Assist those Governments which desire to incorporate these and other environmental factors into national planning processes;

(*d*) Improve the international acceptability of procedures for testing pollutants and contaminants by:

   (i) International division of labour in carrying out the large-scale testing programmes needed;

   (ii) Development of international schedules of tests for evaluation of the environmental impact potential of specific contaminants or products. Such a schedule of tests should include consideration of both short-term and long-term effects of all kinds, and should be reviewed and brought up to date from time to time to take into account new knowledge and techniques;

   (iii) Development and implementation of an international intercalibration programme for sampling and analytical techniques to permit more meaningful comparisons of national data;

   (iv) Develop plans for an International Registry of Data on Chemicals in the Environment based on a collection of available scientific data on the environmental behaviour of the most important man-made chemicals and containing production figures of the potentially most harmful chemicals, together with their pathways from factory *via* utilization to ultimate disposal or recirculation.

Recommendation 75

It is recommended that, without reducing in any way their attention to non-radioactive pollutants, Governments should:

(*a*) Explore with the International Atomic Energy Agency and the World Health Organization the feasibility of developing a registry of releases to the biosphere of significant quantities of radioactive materials;

(*b*) Support and expand, under the International Atomic Energy Agency and appropriate international organizations, international co-operation on radioactive waste problems, including problems of mining and tailings and also including co-ordination of plans for the siting of fuel-reprocessing plants in relation to the siting of the ultimate storage area, considering also the transportation problems.

Recommendation 76

It is recommended:

(*a*) That a major effort be undertaken to develop monitoring and both epidemiological and experimental research programmes providing data for early warning and prevention of the deleterious effects of the various environmental agents, acting singly or in combination, to which man is increasingly exposed, directly or indirectly, and for the assessment of their potential risks to human health, with particular regard to the risks of mutagenicity, teratogenicity and carcinogenicity. Such programmes should be guided and co-ordinated by the World Health Organization;

(*b*) That the World Health Organization co-ordinate the development and implementation of an appropriate international collection and dissemination system to correlate medical, environmental and family-history data;

(*c*) That Governments actively support and contribute to international programmes for research and development of guidelines concerning environmental factors in the work environment.

Recommendation 77

It is recommended that the World Health Organization, in collaboration with the relevant agencies, in the context of an approved programme, and with a view to suggesting necessary action, assist Governments, particularly those of developing countries, in undertaking co-ordinated programmes of monitoring of air and water and in establishing monitoring systems in areas where there may be a risk to health from pollution.

Recommendation 78

It is recommended that internationally co-ordinated programmes of research and monitoring of food contamination by chemical and biological agents be established and developed jointly by the Food and Agriculture Organization of the United Nations and the World Health Organization, taking into account national programmes, and that the results of monitoring be expeditiously assembled, evaluated and made available so as to provide early information on rising trends of contamination and on levels that may be considered undesirable or may lead to unsafe human intakes.

Recommendation 79

It is recommended:

(*a*) That approximately 10 baseline stations be set up, with the consent of the States involved, in areas remote from all sources of pollution in order to monitor long-term global trends in atmospheric constituents and properties which may cause changes in meteorological properties, including climatic changes;

(*b*) That a much larger network of not less than 100 stations be set up, with the consent of the States involved, for monitoring properties and constituents of the atmosphere on a regional basis and especially changes in the distribution and concentration of contaminants;

(c)   That these programmes be guided and co-ordinated by the World Meteorological Organization;

(d)   That the World Meteorological Organization, in co-operation with the International Council of Scientific Unions (ICSU), continue to carry out the Global Atmospheric Research Programme (GARP), and if necessary establish new programmes to understand better the general circulation of the atmosphere and the causes of climatic changes whether these causes are natural or the result of man's activities.

Recommendation 80

It is recommended that the Secretary-General ensure:

(a)   That research activities in terrestrial ecology be encouraged, supported and co-ordinated through the appropriate agencies, so as to provide adequate knowledge of the inputs, movements, residence times and ecological effects of pollutants identified as critical;

(b)   That regional and global networks of existing and, where necessary, new research stations, research centres, and biological reserves be designated or established within the framework of the Man and the Biosphere Programme (MAB) in all major ecological regions, to facilitate intensive analysis of the structure and functioning of ecosystems under natural or managed conditions;

(c)   That the feasibility of using stations participating in this programme for surveillance of the effects of pollutants on ecosystems be investigated;

(d)   That programmes such as the Man and the Biosphere Programme be used to the extent possible to monitor: (i) the accumulation of hazardous compounds in biological and abiotic material at representative sites; (ii) the effect of such accumulation on the reproductive success and population size of selected species.

Recommendation 81

It is recommended that the World Health Organization, together with the international organizations concerned, continue to study, and establish, primary standards for the protection of the human organism, especially from pollutants that are common to air, water and food, as a basis for the establishment of derived working limits.

Recommendation 82

It is recommended that increased support be given to the Codex Alimentarius Commission to develop international standards for pollutants in food and a code of ethics for international food trade, and that the capabilities of the Food and Agriculture Organization of the United Nations and the World Health Organization to assist materially and to guide developing countries in the field of food control be increased.

Recommendation 83

It is recommended that the appropriate United Nations agencies develop agreed procedures for setting derived working limits for common air and water contaminants.

Recommendation 84

It is recommended that Governments make available, through the International Referral System established in pursuance of recommendation 101 of this Conference, such information as may be requested on their pollution research and pollution control activities, including legislative and administrative arrangements, research on more efficient pollution-control technology, and cost-benefit methodology.

Recommendation 85

It is recommended that any mechanism for co-ordinating and stimulating the actions of the different United Nations organs in connexion with environmental problems include among its functions:

(*a*) Development of an internationally accepted procedure for the identification of pollutants of international significance and for the definition of the degree and scope of international concern;

(*b*) Consideration of the appointment of appropriate intergovernmental, expert bodies to assess quantitatively the exposures, risks, pathways and sources of pollutants of international significance;

(*c*) Review and co-ordination of international co-operation for pollution control, ensuring in particular that needed measures shall be taken and that measures taken in regard to various media and sources shall be consistent with one another;

(*d*) Examination of the needs for technical assistance to Governments in the study of pollution problems, in particular those involving international distribution of pollutants;

(*e*) Encouragement of the establishment of consultation mechanisms for speedy implementation of concerted abatement programmes with particular emphasis on regional activities.

B.   MARINE POLLUTION

Recommendation 86

It is recommended that Governments, with the assistance and guidance of appropriate United Nations bodies, in particular the Joint Group of Experts on the Scientific Aspects of Marine Pollution (GESAMP):

(*a*) Accept and implement available instruments on the control of the maritime sources of marine pollution;

(*b*) Ensure that the provisions of such instruments are complied with by ships flying their flags and by ships operating in areas under their jurisdiction and that adequate provisions are made for reviewing the effectiveness of, and revising, existing and proposed international measures for control of marine pollution;

(*c*) Ensure that ocean dumping by their nationals anywhere, or by any person in areas under their jurisdiction, is controlled and that Governments shall continue to work towards the completion of, and bringing into force as soon as possible of, an over-all instrument for the control of ocean dumping as well as needed regional agreements within the framework of this instrument, in particular for enclosed and semi-enclosed seas, which are more at risk from pollution;

(*d*) Refer the draft articles and annexes contained in the report of the intergovernmental meetings at Reykjavik, Iceland, in April 1972 and in London in May 1972 to the United Nations Committee on the Peaceful Uses of the Seabed and the Ocean Floor beyond the Limits of National Jurisdiction at its session in July/August 1972 for information and comments and to a conference of Governments to be convened by the Government of the United Kingdom of Great Britain and Northern Ireland in consultation with the Secretary-General of the United Nations before November 1972 for further consideration, with a view to opening the proposed convention for signature at a place to be decided by that Conference, preferably before the end of 1972;

(e) Participate fully in the 1973 Intergovernmental Maritime Consultative Organization (IMCO) Conference on Marine Pollution and the Conference on the Law of the Sea scheduled to begin in 1973, as well as in regional efforts, with a view to bringing all significant sources of pollution within the marine environment, including radioactive pollution from nuclear surface ships and submarines, and in particular in enclosed and semi-enclosed seas, under appropriate controls and particularly to complete elimination of deliberate pollution by oil from ships, with the goal of achieving this by the middle of the present decade;

(f) Strengthen national controls over land-based sources of marine pollution, in particular in enclosed and semi-enclosed seas, and recognize that, in some circumstances, the discharge of residual heat from nuclear and other power-stations may constitute a potential hazard to marine ecosystems.

Recommendation 87

It is recommended that Governments:

(a) Support national research and monitoring efforts that contribute to agreed international programmes for research and monitoring in the marine environment, in particular the Global Investigation of Pollution in the Marine Environment (GIPME) and the Integrated Global Ocean Station System (IGOSS);

(b) Provide to the United Nations, the Food and Agriculture Organization of the United Nations and the United Nations Conference on Trade and Development, as appropriate to the data-gathering activities of each, statistics on the production and use of toxic or dangerous substances that are potential marine pollutants, especially if they are persistent;

(c) Expand their support to components of the United Nations system concerned with research and monitoring in the marine environment and adopt the measures required to improve the constitutional, financial and operational basis under which the Intergovernmental Oceanographic Commission is at present operating so as to make it an effective joint mechanism for the Governments and United Nations organizations concerned (United Nations Educational, Scientific and Cultural Organization, Food and Agriculture Organization of the United Nations, World Meteorological Organization, Inter-Governmental Maritime Consultative Organization, United Nations) and in order that it may be able to take on additional responsibilities for the promotion and co-ordination of scientific programmes and services.

Recommendation 88

It is recommended that the Secretary-General, together with the sponsoring agencies, make it possible for the Joint Group of Experts on the Scientific Aspects of Marine Pollution (GESAMP):

(a) To re-examine annually, and revise as required, its "Review of Harmful Chemical Substances", with a view to elaborating further its assessment of sources, pathways and resulting risks of marine pollutants;

(b) To assemble, having regard to other work in progress, scientific data and to provide advice on scientific aspects of marine pollution, especially those of an interdisciplinary nature.

Recommendation 89

It is recommended that the Secretary-General ensure:

(*a*) That mechanisms for combining world statistics on mining, production, processing, transport and use of potential marine pollutants shall be developed along with methods for identifying high-priority marine pollutants based in part on such data;

(*b*) That the Joint Group of Experts on the Scientific Aspects of Marine Pollution (GESAMP), in consultation with other expert groups, propose guidelines for test programmes to evaluate toxicity of potential marine pollutants;

(*c*) That the Food and Agriculture Organization of the United Nations, the World Health Organization, the Intergovernmental Oceanographic Commission and the International Atomic Energy Agency encourage studies of the effects of high-priority marine pollutants on man and other organisms, with appropriate emphasis on chronic, low-level exposures;

(*d*) That the Intergovernmental Oceanographic Commission, with the Food and Agriculture Organization of the United Nations and the World Health Organization, explore the possibility of establishing an international institute for tropical marine studies, which would undertake training as well as research.

Recommendation 90

It is recommended that the Intergovernmental Oceanographic Commission, jointly with the World Meteorological Organization and, as appropriate, in cooperation with other interested intergovernmental bodies, promote the monitoring of marine pollution, preferably within the framework of the Integrated Global Ocean Station System (IGOSS), as well as the development of methods for monitoring high-priority marine pollutants in the water, sediments and organisms, with advice from the Joint Group of Experts on the Scientific Aspects of Marine Pollution (GESAMP) on intercomparability of methodologies.

Recommendation 91

It is recommended that the Intergovernmental Oceanographic Commission:

(*a*) Ensure that provision shall be made in international marine research, monitoring and related activities for the exchange, dissemination, and referral to sources of data and information on baselines and on marine pollution and that attention shall be paid to the special needs of developing countries;

(*b*) Give full consideration, with the Food and Agriculture Organization of the United Nations, the World Meteorological Organization, the Inter-Governmental Maritime Consultative Organization, the World Health Organization, the International Atomic Energy Agency, the International Hydrographic Organization and the International Council for the Exploration of the Sea and other interested and relevant organizations, to the strengthening of on-going and related data and information exchange and dissemination activities;

(*c*) Support the concept of development of an interdisciplinary and inter-organizational system primarily involving centres already in existence;

(*d*) Initiate an interdisciplinary marine pollution data and scientific information referral capability.

Recommendation 92

It is recommended:

(*a*) That Governments collectively endorse the principles set forth in paragraph

197 of Conference document A/CONF.48/8[3] as guiding concepts for the Conference on the Law of the Sea and the Inter-Governmental Maritime Consultative Organization (IMCO) Marine Pollution Conference scheduled to be held in 1973 and also the statement of objectives agreed on at the second session of the Intergovernmental Working Group on Marine Pollution, which reads as follows:

> "The marine environment and all the living organisms which it supports are of vital importance to humanity, and all people have an interest in assuring that this environment is so managed that its quality and resources are not impaired. This applies especially to coastal area resources. The capacity of the sea to assimilate wastes and render them harmless and its ability to regenerate natural resources are not unlimited. Proper management is required and measures to prevent and control marine pollution must be regarded as an essential element in this management of the oceans and seas and their natural resources.",

and that, in respect of the particular interest of coastal States in the marine environment and recognizing that the resolution of this question is a matter for consideration at the Conference on the Law of the Sea, they take note of the principles on the rights of coastal States discussed but neither endorsed nor rejected at the second session of the Intergovernmental Working Group on Marine Pollution and refer those principles to the 1973 Inter-Governmental Maritime Consultative Organization Conference for information and to the 1973 Conference on the Law of the Sea for such action as may be appropriate;

(b) That Governments take early action to adopt effective national measures for the control of all significant sources of marine pollution, including land-based sources, and concert and co-ordinate their actions regionally and wher appropriate on a wider international basis;

(c) That the Secretary-General, in co-operation with appropriate international organizations, endeavour to provide guidelines which Governments might wish to take into account when developing such measures.

Recommendation 93

It is recommended that any mechanism for co-ordinating and stimulating the actions of the different United Nations organs in connexion with environmental problems include among its functions over-all responsibility for ensuring that needed advice on marine pollution problems shall be provided to Governments.

Recommendation 94

It is recommended that the Secretary-General, with the co-operation of United Nations bodies, take steps to secure additional financial support to those training and other programmes of assistance that contribute to increasing the capacity of developing countries to participate in international marine research, monitoring and pollution-control programmes.

Educational, informational, social and
cultural aspects of environmental issues

Recommendation 95

It is recommended that the Secretary-General make arrangements for the United Nations system:

(a) To provide countries on request with the necessary technical and financial assistance in preparing national reports on the environment, in setting up ma-

---

3. See annex III.

chinery for monitoring environmental developments from the social and cultural standpoint and, in particular, in drawing up national social, educational and cultural programmes;

(b) To support and encourage projects for continuing co-operation among national social, educational and cultural programmes, including their economic aspects, in an international network. The organizations of the United Nations system, including the regional economic commissions and the United Nations Economic Social Office in Beirut, will be called upon to participate in this activity, as will other international governmental and non-governmental agencies;

(c) To organize the exchange of information on experience, methods and work in progress in connexion with continuous social diagnosis, particularly at the regional level and between regions with common problems;

(d) To facilitate the development of social and cultural indicators for the environment, in order to establish a common methodology for assessing environmental developments and preparing reports on the subject;

(e) To prepare, on the basis of the national reports on the state of, and outlook for, the environment, periodic reports on regional or subregional situations and on the international situation in this matter.

The activities described above could be co-ordinated by the new bodies for environmental co-ordination, taking into account the priorities agreed upon according to the resources available. International bodies responsible for technical and financial co-operation and assistance could also help in carrying out these tasks.

Recommendation 96

1. *It is recommended* that the Secretary-General, the organizations of the United Nations system, especially the United Nations Educational, Scientific and Cultural Organization, and the other international agencies concerned, should, after consultation and agreement, take the necessary steps to establish an international programme in environmental education, interdisciplinary in approach, in school and out of school, encompassing all levels of education and directed towards the general public, in particular the ordinary citizen living in rural and urban areas, youth and adult alike, with a view to educating him as to the simple steps he might take, within his means, to manage and control his environment. A programme of technical and financial co-operation and assistance will be needed to support this programme, taking into account the priorities agreed upon according to the resources available. This programme should include, among other things:

(a) The preparation of an inventory of existing systems of education which include environmental education;

(b) The exchange of information on such systems and, in particular, dissemination of the results of experiments in teaching;

(c) The training and retraining of professional workers in various disciplines at various levels (including teacher training);

(d) Consideration of the formation of groups of experts in environmental disciplines and activities, including those concerning the economic, sociological, tourist and other sectors, in order to facilitate the exchange of experience between countries which have similar environmental conditions and comparable levels of development;

(e) The development and testing of new materials and methods for all types and levels of environmental education.

2. *It is further recommended* that United Nations Educational, Scientific and

Cultural Organization, under the Man and the Biosphere Programme, the World Health Organization, the Food and Agricultural Organization of the United Nations, the United Nations Industrial Development Organization, the World Meteorological Organization and all the organizations concerned, including the scientific unions co-ordinated by the International Council of Scientific Unions, should develop their activities in studying desirable innovations in the training of specialists and technicians and, in collaboration with the United Nations Development Programme, should encourage the institution, at the regional and the international level, of courses and training periods devoted to the environment.

3. *It is further recommended* that international organizations for voluntary service, and, in particular, the International Secretariat for Volunteer Service, should include environmental skills in the services they provide, in consultation with the United Nations Development Programme through the United Nations Volunteer Programme.

Recommendation 97

1. *It is recommended* that the Secretary-General make arrangements:

(a) To establish an information programme designed to create the awareness which individuals should have of environmental issues and to associate the public with environmental management and control. This programme will use traditional and contemporary mass media of communication, taking distinctive national conditions into account. In addition, the programme must provide means of stimulating active participation by the citizens, and of eliciting interest and contributions from non-governmental organizations for the preservation and development of the environment;

(b) To institute the observance of a World Environment Day;

(c) For the preparatory documents and official documents of the Conference to be translated into the widest possible range of languages and circulated as widely as possible;

(d) To integrate relevant information on the environment in all its various aspects into the activities of the information organs of the United Nations system;

(e) To develop technical co-operation, particularly through and between the United Nations regional economic commissions and the United Nations Economic and Social Office in Beirut.

2. *It is also recommended* that the Secretary-General and the development agencies make arrangements to use and adapt certain international development programmes — provided that this can be done without delaying their execution — so as to improve the dissemination of information and to strengthen community action on environment problems, especially among the oppressed and underprivileged peoples of the earth.

Recommendation 98

It is recommended that Governments, with the assistance of the Secretary-General, the Food and Agricultural Organization of the United Nations, the United Nations Educational Scientific and Cultural Organization and the other international and regional intergovernmental and non-governmental agencies concerned, should continue the preparation of the present and future conventions required for the conservation of the world's natural resources and cultural heritage. In the course of this preparatory work, Governments should consider the possibility of putting into operation systems of protection for elements of the world heritage, under which those Governments that wish to save elements of their national heritage of universal value would be able to obtain from the international community, on request, the technical and financial assistance required to bring their efforts to fruition.

Recommendation 99

1. *It is recommended* that Governments should:

(*a*) Noting that the draft convention prepared by United Nations Educational, Scientific and Cultural Organization concerning the protection of the world natural and cultural heritage marks a significant step towards the protection, on an international scale, of the environment, examine this draft convention with a view to its adoption at the next General Conference of UNESCO;

(*b*) Whenever appropriate, sign the Convention on Conservation of Wetlands of International Importance;

2. *It is recommended* that the Secretary-General, in consultation with the competent agencies of the United Nations system and the non-governmental organizations concerned, make arrangements for a detailed study of all possible procedures for protecting certain islands for science;

3. *It is recommended* that a plenipotentiary conference be convened as soon as possible, under appropriate governmental or intergovernmental auspices, to prepare and adopt a convention on export, import and transit of certain species of wild animals and plants.

Recommendation 100

It is recommended that the Secretary-General make arrangements:

(*a*)   To be kept informed of national pilot schemes for new forms of environmental management;

(*b*)   To assist countries, on request, with their research and experiments;

(*c*)   To organize the international exchange of information collected on this subject.

Recommendation 101

It is recommended that the Secretary-General take the appropriate steps, including the convening of an expert meeting, to organize an International Referral Service for sources of environmental information, taking into account the model described in paragraphs 129 to 136 of the report on educational, informational, social and cultural aspects of environmental issues (A/CONF.48/9), in order to assist in the successful implementation of all the recommendations made in respect of those aspects of environmental issues and of most of the recommendations envisaged in the other substantive subject areas covered in the Conference agenda.

Development and environment

Recommendation 102

It is recommended that the appropriate regional organizations give full consideration to the following steps:

(*a*)   Preparing short-term and long-term plans at regional, subregional and sectoral levels for the study and identification of the major environmental problems faced by the countries of the region concerned as well as the special problems of the least developed countries of the region and of countries with coastlines and inland lakes and rivers exposed to the risk of marine and other forms of pollution;

(b) Evaluating the administrative, technical and legal solutions to various environmental problems in terms of both preventive and remedial measures, taking into account possible alternative and/or multidisciplinary approaches to development;

(c) Preparation, within the framework of international agreements, of legislative measures designed to protect marine (and fresh-water) fisheries resources within the limits of their national jurisdiction;

(d) Increasing and facilitating, in the context of development and as proposed in the World Plan of Action for the Application of Science and Technology to Development, the acquisition and distribution of information and experience to member countries through global and regional co-operation, with particular emphasis on an international information referral networks approach and on a regular exchange of information and observation among the regional organizations;

(e) Establishing facilities for the exchange of information and experience between less industrialized countries which, although situated in different regions, share similar problems as a result of common physical, climatic and other factors;

(f) Encouraging the training of personnel in the techniques of incorporating environmental considerations into developmental planning, and of identifying and analyzing the economic and social cost-benefit relationships of alternative approaches;

(g) Establishing criteria, concepts and a terminology of the human environment through interdisciplinary efforts;

(h) Establishing and disseminating information on the significant environmental problems of each region and the nature and result of steps taken to cope with them;

(i) Providing and co-ordinating technical assistance activities directed towards establishing systems of environmental research, information and analysis at the national level;

(j) Assisting developing countries, in co-operation with appropriate international agencies, in promoting elementary education, with emphasis on hygiene, and in developing and applying suitable methods for improving health, housing, sanitation and water supply, and controlling soil erosion. Emphasis should be placed on techniques promoting the use of local labour and utilizing local materials and local expertise in environmental management.

(k) Encouraging the appropriate agencies and bodies within the United Nations to assist the developing countries, at their request, in establishing national science, technology and research policies to enable the developing countries to acquire the capacity to identify and combat environmental problems in the early planning and development stages. In this respect, special priority should be accorded to the type of research, technology and science which would help developing countries speed up, without adverse environment effects, the exploration, exploitation, processing and marketing of their natural resources.

Recommendation 103

It is recommended that Governments take the necessary steps to ensure:

(a) That all countries present at the Conference agree not to invoke environmental concerns as a pretext for discriminatory trade policies or for reduced access to markets and recognize further that the burdens of the environmental policies of the industrialized countries should not be transferred, either directly or indirectly, to the developing countries. As a general rule, no country should solve or disregard its environmental problems at the expense of other countries;

(b) That where environmental concerns lead to restrictions on trade, or to stricter environmental standards with negative effects on exports, particularly from developing countries, appropriate measures for compensation should be worked out within the framework of existing contractual and institutional arrangements and any new such arrangements that can be worked out in the future;

(c) That the General Agreement of Tariffs and Trade, among other international organizations, could be used for the examination of the problems, specifically through the recently established Group on Environmental Measures and International Trade and through its general procedures for bilateral and multilateral adjustment of differences;

(d) That whenever possible (that is, in cases which do not require immediate discontinuation of imports), countries should inform their trading partners in advance about the intended action in order that there might be an opportunity to consult within the GATT Group on Environmental Measures and International Trade, among other international organizations. Assistance in meeting the consequences of stricter environmental standards ought to be given in the form of financial or technical assistance for research with a view to removing the obstacles that the products of developing countries have encountered;

(e) That all countries agree that uniform environmental standards should not be expected to be applied universally by all countries with respect to given industrial processes or products except in those cases where environmental disruption may constitute a concern to other countries. In addition, in order to avoid an impairment of the access of the developing countries to the markets of the industrialized countries because of differential product standards, Governments should aim at world-wide harmonization of such standards. Environmental standards should be established, at whatever levels are necessary, to safeguard the environment, and should not be directed towards gaining trade advantages;

(f) That the Governments and the competent international organizations keep a close watch on medium- and long-term trends in international trade and take measures with a view to promoting:

    (i)   The exchange of environmental protection technologies;

    (ii) International trade in natural products and commodities which compete with synthetic products that have a greater capacity for pollution.

Recommendation 104

It is recommended that the Secretary-General ensure:

(a) That appropriate steps shall be taken by the existing United Nations organizations to identify the major threats to exports, particularly those of developing countries, that arise from environmental concerns, their character and severity, and the remedial action that may be envisaged;

(b) That the United Nations system, in co-operation with other governmental and non-governmental agencies working in this field, should assist Governments to develop mutually acceptable common international environmental standards on products which are considered by Governments to be of significance in foreign trade. Testing and certification procedures designed to ensure that the products conform to these standards should be such as to avoid arbitrary and discriminatory actions that might affect the trade of developing countries.

Recommendation 105

It is recommended that the General Agreement of Tariffs and Trade, the United Nations Conference on Trade and Development and other international bodies, as appropriate, should, within their respective fields of competence, consider undertaking to monitor, assess, and regularly report the emergence of tariff and non-tariff barriers to trade as a result of environmental policies.

Recommendation 106

It is recommended:

(*a*) That the Secretary-General, in co-operation with other international bodies as appropriate, should examine the extent to which the problems of pollution could be ameliorated by a reduction in the current levels of production and in the future rate of growth of the production of synthetic products and substitutes which, in their natural form, could be produced by developing countries; and make recommendations for national and international action;

(*b*) That Governments of the developing countries consider fully the new opportunities that may be offered to them to establish industries and/or expand existing industries in which they may have comparative advantages because of environmental considerations, and that special care be taken to apply the appropriate international standards on environment in order to avoid the creation of pollution problems in developing countries;

(*c*) That the Secretary-General, in consultation with appropriate international agencies, undertake a full review of the practical implications of environmental concerns in relation to distribution of future industrial capacity and, in particular, to ways in which the developing countries may be assisted to take advantage of opportunities and to minimize risks in this area.

Recommendation 107

It is recommended that the Secretary-General, in collaboration with appropriate international agencies, ensure that a study be conducted of appropriate mechanisms for financing international environmental action, taking into account General Assembly resolution 2849 (XXVI).

Recommendation 108

It being recognized that it is in the interest of mankind that the technologies for protecting and improving the environment be employed universally, *it is recommended* that the Secretary-General be asked to undertake studies, in consultation with Governments and appropriate international agencies, to find means by which environmental technologies may be made available for adoption by developing countries under terms and conditions that encourage their wide distribution without constituting an unacceptable burden to developing countries.

Recommendation 109

It is recommended that the Secretary-General, in collaboration with appropriate international agencies, take steps to ensure that the environmental considerations of an international nature related to the foregoing recommendations be integrated into the review and appraisal of the International Development Strategy for the Second Development Decade in such a way that the flow of international aid to developing countries is not hampered. Recommendations for national action, proposed by the Secretary-General of the Conference, shall be referred to Governments for their consideration and, when deemed appropriate, should be taken into account in the review and appraisal process during the consideration of matters for national action as included in the International Development Strategy. It should further be ensured that the preoccupation of developed countries with their own environmental problems should not affect the flow of assistance to developing countries, and that this flow should be adequate to meet the additional environmental requirements of such countries.

C. THE ACTION PLAN

All of the recommendations approved by the Conference for action at the international level (see section B above) are rearranged in the following Action Plan for the Human Environment within the approved framework (see section A above). The recommendations which, before and during the Conference, had been dealt with sectorally, by subject area, are redistributed below, according to function, into the three components of the Action Plan: the global environmental assessment programme (Earthwatch), the environmental management activities, and the supporting measures.

ENVIRONMENTAL ASSESSMENT (EARTHWATCH)

This category includes the functions listed below.

Evaluation and review: to provide the basis for identification of the knowledge needed and to determine that the necessary steps be taken:

Recommendations 4 (1), 11, 14, 18, 41, 48, 54, 55, 60, 61, 62, 63, 70, 73, 74, 75, 81, 85, 88, 91, 92, 94, 95, 106, 109.

Research: to create new knowledge of the kinds specifically needed to provide guidance in the making of decisions:

Recommendations 4, 12 (2), 13, 16, 18, 20, 23, 24, 26, 28, 41, 42, 43, 44, 45, 48, 49, 51, 52, 53, 59, 62, 64, 65, 66, 68, 73, 76, 78, 79, 80, 84, 87, 88, 89, 94, 95, 102, 106, 108.

Monitoring: to gather certain data on specific environmental variables and to evaluate such data in order to determine and predict important environmental conditions and trends:

Recommendations 18, 25, 29, 30, 40, 46, 51, 55, 57, 67, 73, 74, 76, 77, 78, 79, 80, 87, 90, 91, 94, 95, 105.

Information exchange: to disseminate knowledge within the scientific and technological communities and to ensure that decision-makers at all levels shall have the benefit of the best knowledge that can be made available in the forms and at the times in which it can be useful:

Recommendations 2, 4 (2), 5, 16, 19, 20, 26, 27, 35, 41, 45, 46, 49, 51, 52, 53, 56, 58, 74, 84, 91, 95, 96 (1), 97 (2), 100, 101, 102.

ENVIRONMENTAL MANAGEMENT

This category covers functions designed to facilitate comprehensive planning that takes into account the side effects of man's activities and thereby to protect and enhance the human environment for present and future generations.

Recommendations 1, 2, 3, 9, 12, 13, 14, 15, 17, 18 (3), 18 (4), 19, 21, 22, 23, 27, 32, 33, 36, 37, 38, 39, 42, 43, 44, 45, 46, 47, 48, 50, 51, 52, 53, 54, 55, 61, 63, 68, 69, 70, 71, 72, 75, 81, 82, 83, 84, 85, 86, 92, 93, 94, 96 (3), 98, 99, 102, 103, 104, 105, 106, 108, 109.

SUPPORTING MEASURES

This category relates to measures required for the activities in the other two categories (environmental assessment and environmental management).

Education, training and public information: to supply needed specialists, multi-disciplinary professionals and technical personnel an dto facilitate the use of knowledge in decision-making at every level.

Recommendations 6, 7, 8, 13, 16, 19, 31, 34, 73, 89, 94, 96, 97, 102.

Organizational arrangements

Recommendations 4 (1), 7, 16, 17, 18 (4), 23, 31, 33, 41, 42, 43, 45, 49, 50, 51, 52, 85, 87, 93, 101, 102.

Financial and other forms of assistance

Recommendations 1, 10, 16, 17, 18 (3), 18 (4), 42, 43 (6), 45, 49, 50, 53, 73, 87, 94, 95, 96, 107.

Institutional and financial arrangements for international environmental co-operation

The General Assembly,

Convinced of the need for prompt and effective implementation by Governments and the international community of measures designed to safeguard and enhance the human environment for the benefit of present and future generations of man,

Recognizing that responsibility for action to protect and enhance the human environment rests primarily with Governments and, in the first instance, can be exercised more effectively at the national and regional levels,

Recognizing further that environmental problems of broad international significance fall within the competence of the United Nations system,

Bearing in mind that international co-operative programmes in the environment field must be undertaken with due respect to the sovereign rights of States and in conformity with the Charter of the United Nations and principles of international law,

Mindful of the sectoral responsibilities of the organizations of the United Nations system,

Conscious of the significance of regional and subregional co-operation in the field of the human environment and of the important role of the regional economic commissions and other regional intergovernmental organizations,

Emphasizing that problems of the human environment constitute a new and important area for international co-operation and that the complexity and interdependence of such problems require new approaches,

Recognizing that the relevant international scientific and other professional communities can make an important contribution to international co-operation in the field of the human environment,

Conscious of the need for processes within the United Nations system which would effectively assist developing countries to implement environmental policies and programmes that are compatible with their development plans and to participate meaningfully in international environmental programmes,

Convinced that, in order to be effective, international co-operation in the field of the human environment requires additional financial and technical resources,

Aware of the urgent need for a permanent institutional arrangement within the United Nations for the protection and improvement of the human environment,

Taking note of the report of the Secretary-General on the United Nations Conference on the Human Environment.

I

Governing Council for Environmental Programmes

1. *Decides* to establish a Governing Council for Environmental Programmes composed of 58 members elected by the General Assembly for three-year terms on the following basis:

(*a*) Sixteen seats for African States;

(*b*) Thirteen seats for Asian States;

(*c*) Ten seats for Latin American States;

(*d*) Thirteen seats for Western European and other States;

(*e*) Six seats for Eastern European States;

2. *Decides* that the Governing Council shall have the following main functions and responsibilities:

(*a*) To promote international co-operation in the environment field and to recommend, as appropriate, policies to this end;

(*b*) To provide general policy guidance for the direction and co-ordination of environmental programmes within the United Nations system;

(*c*) To receive and review the periodic reports of the Executive Director, referred to in section II, paragraph 1, below, on the implementation of environmental programmes within the United Nations system;

(*d*) To keep under review the world environmental situation in order to ensure that emerging environmental problems of wide international significance receive appropriate and adequate consideration by Governments;

(*e*) To promote the contribution of the relevant international scientific and other professional communities to the acquisition, assessment and exchange of environmental knowledge and information and, as appropriate, to the technical aspects of the formulation and implementation of environmental programmes within the United Nations system;

(*f*) To maintain under continuing review the impact of national and international environmental policies and measures on developing countries, as well as the problem of additional costs that may be incurred by developing countries in the implementation of environmental programmes and projects, and to ensure that such programmes and projects shall be compatible with the development plans and priorities of those countries;

(*g*) To review and approve annually the programme of utilization of resources of the Environment Fund referred to in section III below;

3. *Decides* that the Governing Council shall report annually to the General Assembly through the Economic and Social Council, which will transmit to the Assembly such comments on the report as it may deem necessary, particularly with regard to questions of co-ordination and to the relationship of environment policies and programmes within the United Nations system to over-all economic and social policies and priorities.

II

Environment secretariat

1. *Decides* that a small secretariat shall be established in the United Nations to serve as a focal point for environmental action and co-ordination within the United Nations system in such a way as to ensure a high degree of effective management;

2. *Decides* that the environment secretariat shall be headed by the Executive Director, who shall be elected by the General Assembly on the nomination of the Secretary-General for a term of four years and who shall be entrusted, *inter alia*, with the following responsibilities:

(a) To provide substantive support to the Governing Council;

(b) To co-ordinate, under the guidance of the Governing Council, environment programmes within the United Nations system, to keep their implementation under review and to assess their effectiveness;

(c) To advise, as appropriate and under the guidance of the Governing Council, intergovernmental bodies of the United Nations system on the formulation and implementation of environmental programmes;

(d) To secure the effective co-operation of, and contribution from, the relevant scientific and other professional communities from all parts of the world;

(e) To provide, at the request of all parties concerned, advisory services for the promotion of international co-operation in the field of the environment;

(f) To submit to the Governing Council, on his own initiative or upon request, proposals embodying medium-range and long-range planning for United Nations programmes in the field of the environment;

(g) To bring to the attention of the Governing Council any matter which he deems to require consideration by it;

(h) To administer, under the authority and policy guidance of the Governing Council, the Environment Fund referred to in section III below;

(i) To report on environment matters to the Governing Council;

(j) To perform such other functions as may be entrusted to him by the Governing Council;

3. *Decides* that the costs of servicing the Governing Council and providing the small secretariat referred to in paragraph 1 above shall be borne by the regular budget of the United Nations and that operational programme costs, programme support and administrative costs of the Environment Fund established under section III below shall be borne by the Fund.

III

Environment Fund

1. *Decides* that, in order to provide for additional financing for environmental programmes, a voluntary fund shall be established, with effect from 1 January 1973, in accordance with existing United Nations financial procedures;

2. *Decides* that, in order to enable the Governing Council to fulfil its policy-guidance role for the direction and co-ordination of environmental activities, the Environment Fund shall finance wholly or partly the costs of the new environmental initiatives undertaken within the United Nations system — which will include the initiatives envisaged in the Action Plan for the Human Environment adopted by

the United Nations Conference on the Human Environment, with particular attention to integrated projects, and such other environmental activities as may be decided upon by the Governing Council — and that the Governing Council shall review these initiatives with a view to taking appropriate decisions as to their continued financing;

3. *Decides* that the Environment Fund shall be used for financing such programmes of general interest as regional and global monitoring, assessment and data-collecting systems, including, as appropriate, costs for national counterparts; the improvement of environmental quality management; environmental research; information exchange and dissemination; public education and training; assistance for national, regional and global environmental institutions; the promotion of environmental research and studies for the development of industrial and other technologies best suited to a policy of economic growth compatible with adequate environmental safeguards; and such other programmes as the Governing Council may decide upon; and that in the implementation of such programmes due account should be taken of the special needs of the developing countries;

4. *Decides* that, in order to ensure that the development priorities of developing countries shall not be adversely affected, adequate measures shall be taken to provide additional financial resources on terms compatible with the economic situation of the recipient developing country, and that, to this end, the Executive Director, in co-operation with competent organizations, shall keep this problem under continuing review;

5. *Decides* that the Environment Fund, in pursuance of the objectives stated in paragraphs 2 and 3 above, shall be directed to the need for effective co-ordination in the implementation of international environmental programmes of the organizations of the United Nations system and other international organizations;

6. *Decides* that, in the implementation of programmes to be financed by the Environment Fund, organizations outside the United Nations system, particularly those in the countries and regions concerned, shall also be utilized as appropriate, in accordance with the procedures established by the Governing Council, and that such organizations are invited to support the United Nations environmental programmes by complementary initiatives and contributions;

7. *Decides* that the Governing Council shall formulate such general procedures as are necessary to govern the operations of the Environment Fund.

IV

Co-ordination

1. *Decides* that, in order to provide for the most efficient co-ordination of United Nations environmental programmes, an Environmental Co-ordinating Board, under the chairmanship of the Executive Director, should be established under the auspices and within the framework of the Administrative Committee on Co-ordination;

2. *Decides further* that the Environmental Co-ordinating Board shall meet periodically for the purpose of ensuring co-operation and co-ordination among all bodies concerned in the implementation of environmental programmes and that it shall report annually to the Governing Council;

3. *Invites* the organizations of the United Nations system to adopt the measures that may be required to undertake concerted and co-ordinated programmes with

regard to international environmental problems, taking into account existing procedures for prior consultation, particularly on programme and budgetary matters;

4. *Invites* the regional economic commissions and the Economic and Social Office at Beirut, in co-operation where necessary with other appropriate regional bodies, to intensify further their efforts directed towards contributing to the implementation of environmental programmes in view of the particular need for the rapid development of regional co-operation in this field;

5. *Also invites* other intergovernmental and those non-governmental organizations that have an interest in the field of the environment to lend their full support and collaboration to the United Nations with a view to achieving the largest possible degree of co-operation and co-ordination;

6. *Calls upon* Governments to ensure that appropriate national institutions shall be entrusted with the task of the co-ordination of environmental action, both national and international;

7. *Decides* to review as appropriate, at its thirty-first session, the above institutional arrangements, bearing in mind, *inter alia*, the responsibilities of the Economic and Social Council under the Charter of the United Nations.

Index